**Illustrators**
Mike Atkinson, Jim Dugdale, Ron Jobson, Janos Marffy,
John Marshall, Roger Payne, Bernard Robinson,
Mike Saunders, Frederick St. Ward, David Wright

# MY BOOK OF KNOWLEDGE

CLIVEDEN PRESS

# Contents

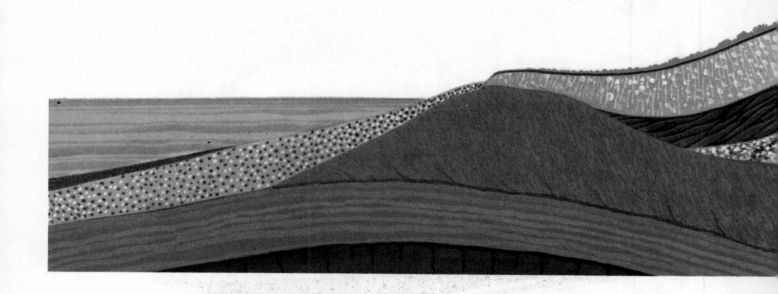

# The Planet Earth

Our planet Earth is like a huge spaceship hurtling through space. It travels at over 100,000 km/h around the Sun, completing an orbit in just over 365 days (one year). At the same time, along with the rest of the Solar System, it travels around the centre of the Milky Way galaxy, taking about 200 million years to complete one of these vast journeys. The Earth also moves in a third way because it spins on its axis, making one turn every 24 hours (one day).

### The Seasons

The axis is an imaginary line running through the centre of the Earth, joining the North and South Poles. It is tilted by about $23\frac{1}{2}$ degrees from the upright. This means that as the Earth orbits the Sun, at certain times of the year the northern half of the Earth, or *northern hemisphere*, is tilted towards the Sun, and the *southern hemisphere* tilted away from it. As a result, the northern hemisphere gets more sunlight than the southern and so is warmer; it is summer in the north and winter in the south. At other times, the southern hemisphere is tilted towards the Sun and the northern hemisphere away from it; it is then summer in the south.

Below: An eclipse of the Sun occurs when the Moon is between the Sun and the Earth and a shadow of the Moon is cast onto the Earth's surface. The picture on the left shows a total eclipse of the Sun, with the Sun's atmosphere revealed.

Total eclipse of the Sun

Earth

Moon

Sun's ray

Below: On June 21, the northern hemisphere leans towards the Sun. It is summer in the northern hemisphere and winter in the south. The opposite occurs on December 21, when it is winter in the northern hemisphere and summer in the south. On September 23 and March 21, sunlight is divided equally between the two hemispheres.

Summer June 21

Autumn September 23

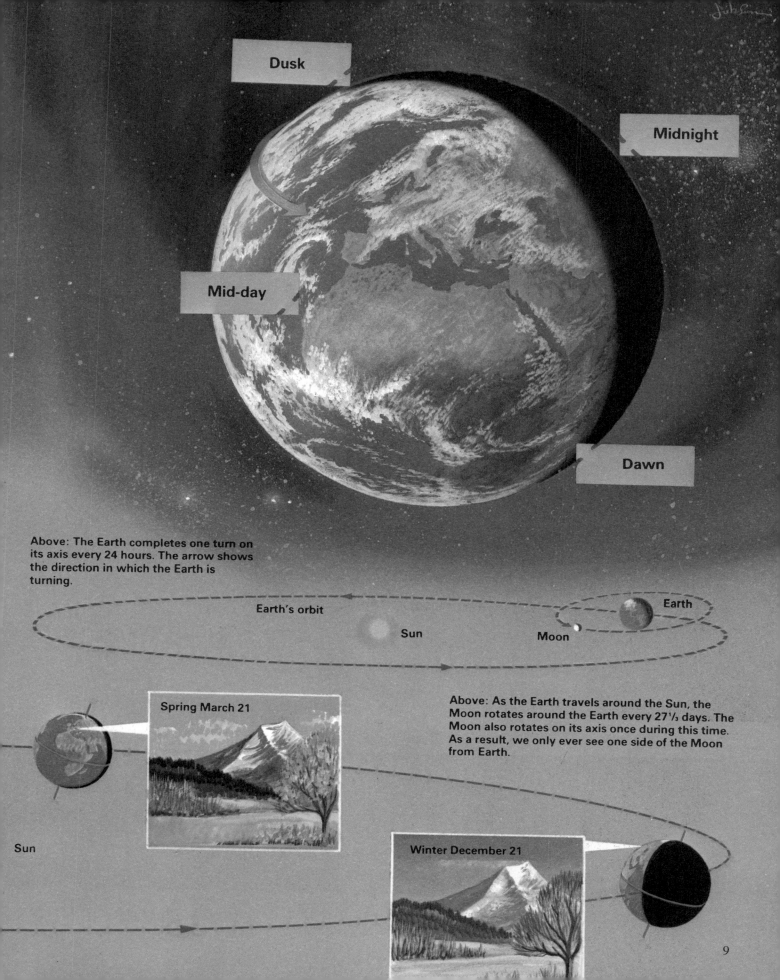

Dusk

Midnight

Mid-day

Dawn

Above: The Earth completes one turn on its axis every 24 hours. The arrow shows the direction in which the Earth is turning.

Earth's orbit

Sun

Moon

Earth

Spring March 21

Above: As the Earth travels around the Sun, the Moon rotates around the Earth every 27⅓ days. The Moon also rotates on its axis once during this time. As a result, we only ever see one side of the Moon from Earth.

Sun

Winter December 21

9

Sun     Mercury     Venus     Earth     Mars     Jupiter

**POLAR CAPS ON MARS**

Winter

Summer

# Family of the Sun

Our Sun, like the millions of stars that twinkle in the night sky, is a glowing ball of hot gases. Nine planets, many of them with their own moons, orbit the Sun. The Earth is one such planet. Some planets, such as Earth and Mars, are rocky, while others, such as Jupiter and Saturn, are giant balls of gas. The Sun and the planets form the Solar System, along with asteroids (small, rocky bodies), comets (streams of dust and gas) and meteorites. Shooting stars are meteorites burning up as they enter the Earth's atmosphere.

Above: A view of Saturn from one of its twenty or more moons, Tethys. Space probes have sent back much information about Saturn and its moons and rings. Above right: Mars has polar caps made of the frozen gas carbon dioxide. The caps melt in summer. Below: The Solar System.

| Planet | Number of Moons | Distance from Sun, average in millions km | Diameter (equator) in km | Length of day | Length of year |
|---|---|---|---|---|---|
| Mercury | 0 | 58 | 4,878 | 176 days | 88 days |
| Venus | 0 | 108 | 12,104 | 2,760 days | 225 days |
| Earth | 1 | 149½ | 12,756 | 24 hours | 365 days |
| Mars | 2 | 228 | 6,794 | 24.6 hours | 687 days |
| Jupiter | 16 | 778½ | 142,800 | 9.8 hours | 11.9 years |
| Saturn | 20? | 1,427 | 120,000 | 10.2 hours | 29.5 years |
| Uranus | 15 | 2,735 | 52,398 | 24 hours | 84 years |
| Neptune | 8 | 4,497 | 48,000? | 22 hours? | 165 years |
| Pluto | 1 | 5,900 | 3,058 | 6.4 hours | 248 years |

Saturn

Uranus

Neptune

Pluto

# Stars and Galaxies

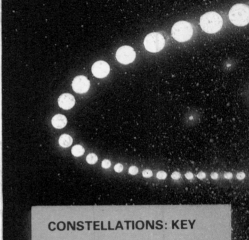

Our Sun is one of 100,000 million stars in the Milky Way galaxy. Galaxies of stars are held together by gravity. Most galaxies are spiral in shape, like the Milky Way galaxy shown on the next page. The Milky Way galaxy measures 100,000 light years across, but it is only one of millions of galaxies in the Universe.

Scientists believe that stars form from clouds of hydrogen, other gases and dust. Gradually, gases are drawn towards the centre, which becomes hot and glows. Nuclear reactions, caused when hydrogen is changed into another gas, helium, create enormous energy. Soon a new star is born, with a surface temperature of 6,000°C. Our Sun is a medium-sized star. Its diameter is 1.4 million km, 109 times the size of Earth.

## Death of a Star

Stars last many millions of years, but eventually the hydrogen supply runs down, and the core of helium starts to collapse. This causes great heating and the outer parts of the star swell up like a balloon, creating a red giant star. When our Sun becomes a red giant, it will swallow up Mercury and Venus, and possibly Earth too. But this will not happen for 5,000 million years. At last, the red giant shrinks to become an Earth-sized, cold, white dwarf star.

**CONSTELLATIONS: KEY**

**Northern Hemisphere**
1 Pegasus, Flying Horse
2 Cygnus, Swan
3 Hercules, Kneeling Giant
4 Boötes, Herdsman
5 Ursa Major, Great Bear
6 Leo, Lion
7 Gemini, Twins
8 Orion, Hunter
9 Perseus, Champion
10 Polaris, Pole Star
11 Ursa Minor, Little Bear

**Southern Hemisphere**
12 Cetus, Sea Monster
13 Orion, Hunter
14 Lepus, Hare
15 Vela, Sails
16 Crater, Cup
17 Crux, Southern Cross
18 Lupus, Wolf
19 Scorpio, Scorpion
20 Sagittarius, Archer
21 Capricornus, Sea Goat
22 Phoenix, Phoenix

**Below: Star charts of the northern hemisphere, left, and the southern hemisphere, right, show star constellations. There are 88** constellations in all. They are named after people, animals and objects and each has a Latin and an English name. (See key, right.)

**Northern Hemisphere**

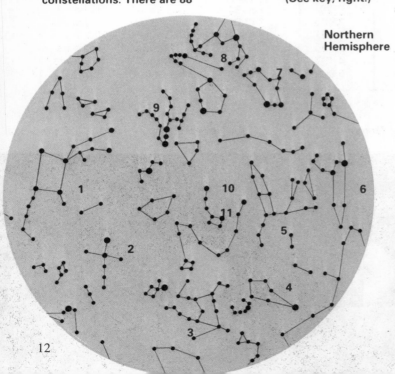

**Southern Hemisphere**

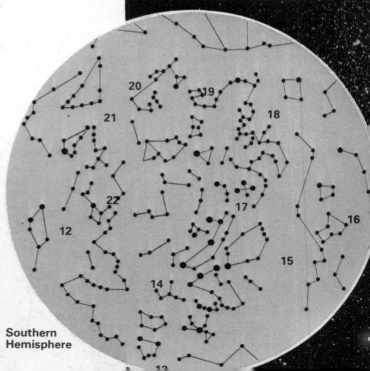

Top: The arrow shows our Sun, which is about two-thirds of the way from the centre of the Milky Way galaxy.
Above: The Crab nebula is the remains of an extremely big star which has blown up to create a glowing mass called a supernova.

The large diagram shows the life of a medium-sized star. Near the top of the page, a star forms from a cloud of gas and dust. The arrow shows the present state of our Sun. After millions of years, the star swells up to form a red giant, right. Much material is lost to space. The core then shrinks into a white dwarf star, below.

# The Moon

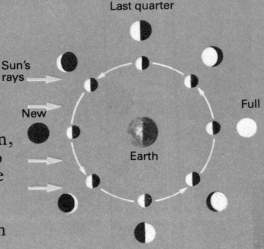

Last quarter

Sun's rays →

New

Earth

Full

First quarter

The Moon is our nearest neighbour in space. It travels around the Earth at a speed of about 3,664 kilometres per hour. It orbits the Earth once every month or so. The Moon, like the Earth, is constantly spinning. It takes it a month to complete one spin. This means that we always see the same face of the Moon from Earth.

When the night sky is clear, we are often surprised how brightly the Moon shines. But the Moon doesn't shine with its own light. It is merely reflecting light from the Sun. Astronauts on the Moon see Earth as a big ball of light. Again, the light from Earth is only reflected sunlight.

Seen from Earth, the Moon looks about the same size as the Sun. But this is only because the Moon is so close to us. In fact, the Moon is quite small – about the same size as Australia. It is so small that it does not have enough gravity to hold an atmosphere around it. There is no air on the Moon, so spacemen have to take their own air with them. And the Moon has no weather – no wind. During the day, the Sun beats down with an intense heat of about 120°C – hotter than boiling water. During the lunar night, the temperature falls to a freezing −160°C.

**The Moon goes through a 29½-day cycle of 'phases' as it circles the Earth. These phases happen because we see only the half of the Moon that is illuminated by the Sun. At New Moon, the Moon cannot be seen because its dark face is turned towards the Earth. After two or three days, it has moved far enough to be seen as a thin crescent in the sky. After seven days it is a perfect half circle called the First Quarter. A week later it is full. We see the full sunlit circle as it lies opposite the Sun in the sky. After this, the phases go into reverse – the Moon wanes until it disappears once more.**

Sun's rays

Moon

Shadow

Earth

It is strange that the Sun and Moon appear in the sky to be the same size although the Moon is really 400 times smaller. It is just much closer to us. The Moon sometimes passes in front of the Sun, blotting out the Sun's light. This is a *solar eclipse.* The Moon's shadow is a cone, as you can see in the picture. To see a total eclipse we must be inside that cone. When the tip of the shadow cone reaches Earth it is only about 240 kilometres across. It is only in this 240 km-wide circle that people see a total eclipse of the Sun.

The Moon has many of the valuable minerals that are becoming scarcer and scarcer on Earth. Perhaps in years to come the Moon's minerals will be mined and transported as in the picture below. Lunar gravity is only one-sixth of Earth's, so it is much easier to shoot things off its surface into space. The minerals could be put in huge buckets and fired off a track by magnetic waves. This mechanism is called a mass driver. Out in space, the minerals could be 'caught' by a space tug (right) and taken to wherever they are needed.

# Exploring Space

The Space Age began in 1957, when the Russians launched a satellite called Sputnik 1. Although it was little larger than a football, it was the first artificial satellite to orbit the Earth. This great achievement caused much rivalry between Russia and the USA. Both countries have had many successes. Russia was the first to send a man into space. The USA was the first to put people on the Moon. The work of these countries has greatly increased our knowledge of the Solar System. Research continues as space probes now reach out to the edge of the Solar System.

## Life in Space

One of the aims of space research has been to discover whether life exists on other planets. We now know that there is no life on the Moon, which does not have any air. And so far, no proof has been found of life anywhere else in the Solar System, not even on our red neighbour, Mars. But scientists estimate that there are 130 solar systems in our part of the Milky Way galaxy. Some of these systems may contain planets much like the Earth. But the nearest star to the Sun is more than four light-years away. A light-year is nearly 10 million million kilometres. Four light-years is more than 3,000 times the distance across the Solar System.

The building of space stations has enabled much scientific work to be carried out. These stations have also shown that people can live in space without harmful effects. For example, two Russian cosmonauts spent 211 days in the Salyut 7 orbiting station in 1982 before returning to Earth. Their experience is helping designers to plan space colonies. These may one day house 10,000 or more people.

**Space shuttle**

**Above: Shuttle spacecraft are designed to take people and materials into space and then return to Earth. The materials will be used to build large space stations.**

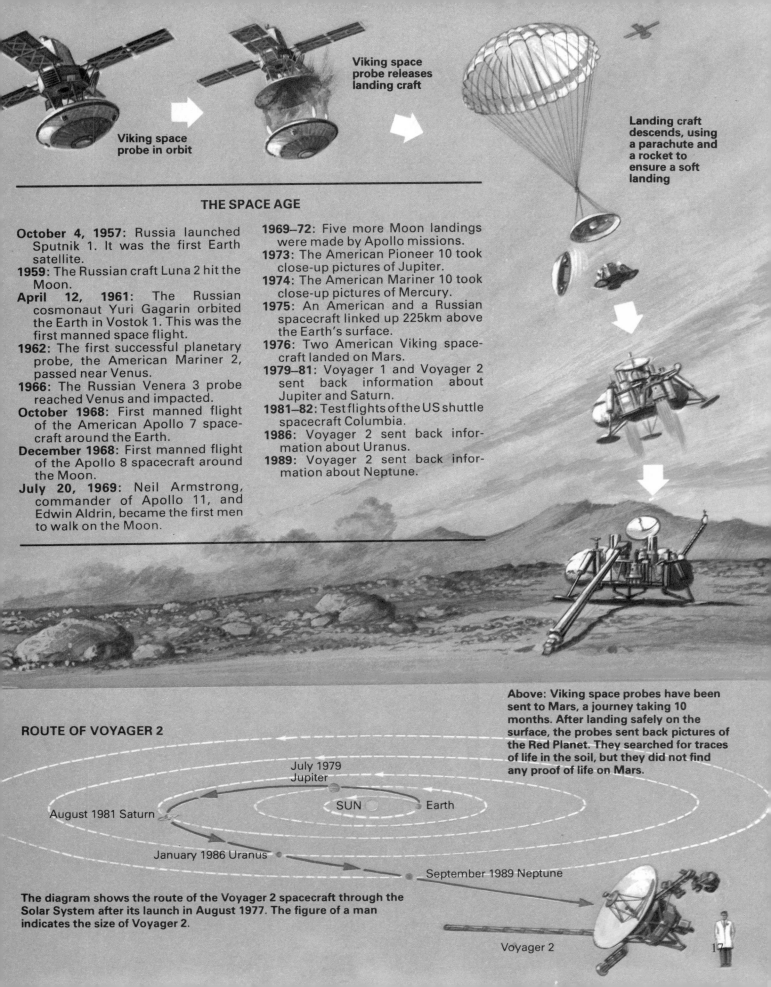

Viking space probe in orbit

Viking space probe releases landing craft

Landing craft descends, using a parachute and a rocket to ensure a soft landing

# THE SPACE AGE

**October 4, 1957:** Russia launched Sputnik 1. It was the first Earth satellite.

**1959:** The Russian craft Luna 2 hit the Moon.

**April 12, 1961:** The Russian cosmonaut Yuri Gagarin orbited the Earth in Vostok 1. This was the first manned space flight.

**1962:** The first successful planetary probe, the American Mariner 2, passed near Venus.

**1966:** The Russian Venera 3 probe reached Venus and impacted.

**October 1968:** First manned flight of the American Apollo 7 spacecraft around the Earth.

**December 1968:** First manned flight of the Apollo 8 spacecraft around the Moon.

**July 20, 1969:** Neil Armstrong, commander of Apollo 11, and Edwin Aldrin, became the first men to walk on the Moon.

**1969–72:** Five more Moon landings were made by Apollo missions.

**1973:** The American Pioneer 10 took close-up pictures of Jupiter.

**1974:** The American Mariner 10 took close-up pictures of Mercury.

**1975:** An American and a Russian spacecraft linked up 225km above the Earth's surface.

**1976:** Two American Viking spacecraft landed on Mars.

**1979–81:** Voyager 1 and Voyager 2 sent back information about Jupiter and Saturn.

**1981–82:** Test flights of the US shuttle spacecraft Columbia.

**1986:** Voyager 2 sent back information about Uranus.

**1989:** Voyager 2 sent back information about Neptune.

Above: Viking space probes have been sent to Mars, a journey taking 10 months. After landing safely on the surface, the probes sent back pictures of the Red Planet. They searched for traces of life in the soil, but they did not find any proof of life on Mars.

## ROUTE OF VOYAGER 2

July 1979 Jupiter

August 1981 Saturn

January 1986 Uranus

SUN    Earth

September 1989 Neptune

The diagram shows the route of the Voyager 2 spacecraft through the Solar System after its launch in August 1977. The figure of a man indicates the size of Voyager 2.

Voyager 2

# Cities in Space

The biggest problem to face the world within the next few decades may be how to feed and house all its people. The world's population is growing fast, especially in Third World countries. Before the year 2080 the population of our Earth may be three times its present size. Unless we can halt the population explosion and find new sources of food and raw materials, people may have to move out into space.

There have been many designs for giant space colonies with room for thousands of people. These colonies would be vast cylinders or spheres, going round and round to give Earth-like gravity for the people who live there.

## Island Three

One idea for a space colony is called *Island Three*. It would be made up of two or more huge cylinders positioned at a fixed distance from the Earth and Moon. The cylinders are 30 kilometres long and about 6 kilometres around. Giant mirrors reflect sunlight through three long windows in the sides of the cylinders. The angle of the mirrors can be altered to make artificial day and night and temperature changes. Even changing seasons can be created. Inside the cylinders will be three long land areas where people live and grow crops, just as they would on Earth.

*Island Three* will have a solar power station at one end and a ring of factory units at the other. There will also be vast docking facilities for spaceships.

## Artificial Gravity

To make life possible for people who go to live in space, there must be gravity. Gravity is the force that pulls us all towards the centre of the Earth – that gives us weight. Out in space there is no gravity. People and things just float around.

*Island Three*

Artificial gravity can be made by spinning a whole space colony at just the right speed. The force of the spin pushes everything towards the outside. To anyone in a space colony, 'up' will be towards the inside. Two people on opposite sides of the craft will be upside down in relation to each other.

## A Torus Colony

Another idea for a space colony is the building of a huge torus or wheel, like the one shown here. The wheel is rotated around the central hub once every minute. This creates an artificial gravity that holds all the land, water and people in place inside the vast tube. The tube itself is 2000 metres across. On the central hub is a solar power station that provides energy to run the whole colony. Also in the hub are factories where many of the colonists work, perhaps using materials mined on the Moon. Life in the tube would be made as much like life on Earth as possible for the colonists.

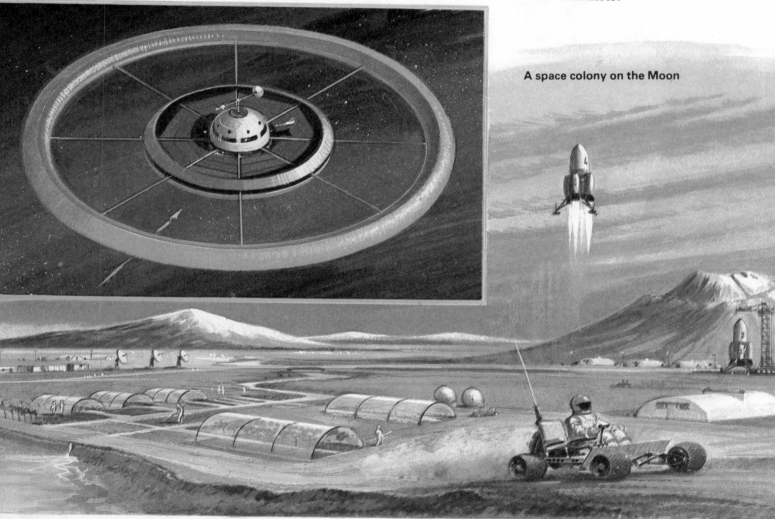

A space colony on the Moon

## Will we go to other Stars?

In the future, people may be able to go to other star systems outside our Solar System. But at present we do not know how it will be possible. The nearest star to us, other than our Sun, is Alpha Centauri, and it would take a present-day rocket ship about 100,000 years to get there! So we will have to develop much faster rocket engines than those we have at present.

But we will almost certainly begin by putting people on other planets and moons in our Solar System. The picture above shows a colony on the Moon. Life will not be too easy for the first settlers. It will take them some time to get used to the very small gravity and the need to carry their own air around with them. Water will either have to be imported from Earth or manufactured on the Moon. Food will be grown in large greenhouses.

# A World of Atoms

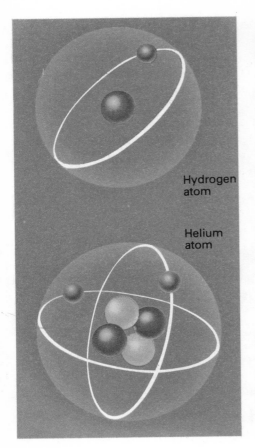

Hydrogen atom

Helium atom

Everything in the universe is made up of atoms. Rocks, water, the air we breathe, plants, animals and people all contain millions upon millions of these tiny, invisible particles. About 30 million atoms placed side by side would stretch across the head of a pin.

But even the tiny atom is made up of even smaller pieces. The simplest atom is that of the light gas hydrogen. At the centre of the hydrogen atom is a tiny solid body called a *proton*. Around this spins an even smaller *electron*. The whirling electron makes billions of trips around the proton in a millionth of a second. Protons have a positive electric charge, electrons have a negative charge.

Other atoms are much more complicated than the hydrogen atom. An atom of another light gas, helium, has two protons, two electrons and there are two particles called *neutrons* with the protons at the centre or *nucleus* of the atom. Neutrons have no electrical charge. The most complicated atom is the uranium atom. It has 92 electrons, 92 protons and 146 neutrons.

**Atoms are so small that if an atom were the size of a finger nail, then your hand would be big enough to grasp the Earth.**

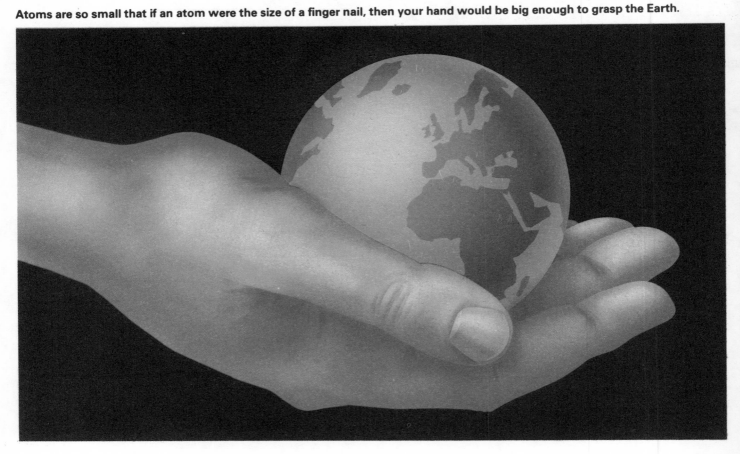

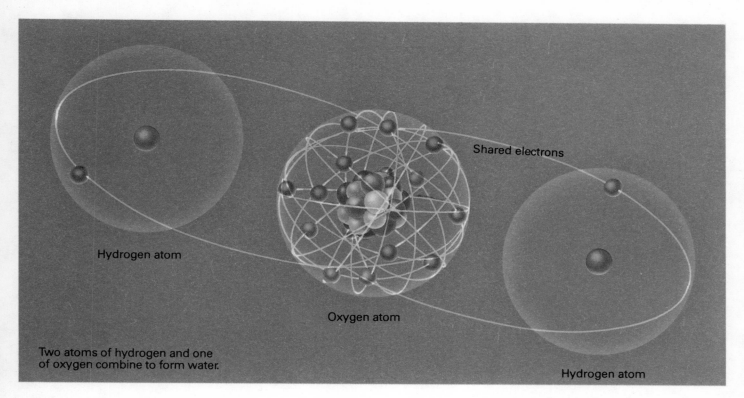

Shared electrons

Hydrogen atom

Oxygen atom

Hydrogen atom

Two atoms of hydrogen and one of oxygen combine to form water.

## The Elements

All the millions of substances in the world are made up from about a hundred simple substances called *elements*. Gold, silver and copper are elements; so are the gases hydrogen and oxygen. The atoms of different elements often join up to make different substances called *compounds*. The salt you put on your food is made up of atoms of the elements sodium and chlorine. Two atoms of hydrogen and one atom of oxygen join to make a *molecule* of water. A molecule is the smallest portion of a substance that can exist.

Every molecule of a substance is made up of the same number of atoms, joined together in exactly the same pattern. The main difference between the atoms of one element and those of another is in the number of protons in the nucleus. For example, every atom of aluminium has 13 protons; every atom of lead has 82. If an atom gains or loses protons, it becomes an atom of another element. The number of protons is called the *atomic number* of the element.

Although there are about a hundred elements, nearly all of the Earth's crust, the atmosphere and the oceans is made up of only eight elements. These are oxygen, the most common, aluminium, silicon, iron, calcium, potassium, sodium and magnesium. In the whole universe, there is more hydrogen than any other element. This is because the stars are made of hydrogen.

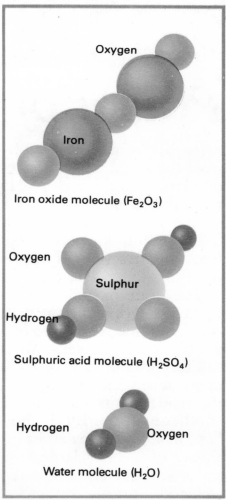

Oxygen

Iron

Iron oxide molecule ($Fe_2O_3$)

Oxygen

Sulphur

Hydrogen

Sulphuric acid molecule ($H_2SO_4$)

Hydrogen

Oxygen

Water molecule ($H_2O$)

# *Power of the Atom*

Scientists have discovered how to get vast amounts of power from the atom. This knowledge can be used for the good of mankind – to make electricity. It can also be used to make nuclear weapons.

The nucleus (centre) of the atom is made up of particles called protons and neutrons, held together by powerful forces of attraction. When the nucleus is broken apart, these forces are released as energy in the form of radiation.

The atoms of some elements are constantly breaking up by themselves. They are called *radioactive elements*. Uranium is one of these. One kind of uranium has 92 protons and 143 neutrons in its nucleus. We add these numbers together and call this uranium 235 or U-235 for short. In U-235, a neutron sometimes shoots off from the nucleus. Sometimes this neutron hits another U-235 neutron and knocks loose another neutron. If this should happen often enough we have a *chain reaction* and a great deal of energy is let loose. If a piece of U-235 is large enough, a great many neutrons fly about at once. The reaction gets out of hand and we have a tremendous explosion – an atomic bomb.

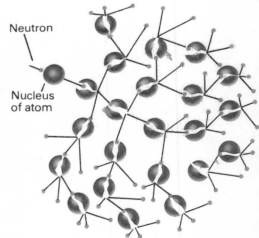

A chain reaction occurs when a neutron splits a uranium atom and produces at least two more neutrons which in turn split other atoms. An uncontrolled chain reaction produces a nuclear explosion.

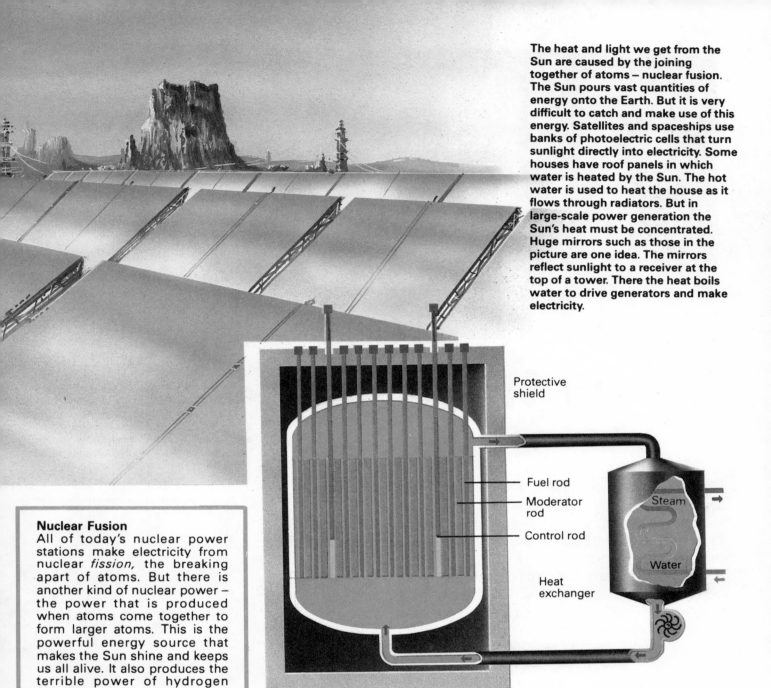

The heat and light we get from the Sun are caused by the joining together of atoms – nuclear fusion. The Sun pours vast quantities of energy onto the Earth. But it is very difficult to catch and make use of this energy. Satellites and spaceships use banks of photoelectric cells that turn sunlight directly into electricity. Some houses have roof panels in which water is heated by the Sun. The hot water is used to heat the house as it flows through radiators. But in large-scale power generation the Sun's heat must be concentrated. Huge mirrors such as those in the picture are one idea. The mirrors reflect sunlight to a receiver at the top of a tower. There the heat boils water to drive generators and make electricity.

Protective shield

Fuel rod

Moderator rod

Control rod

Heat exchanger

Steam

Water

## Nuclear Fusion

All of today's nuclear power stations make electricity from nuclear *fission*, the breaking apart of atoms. But there is another kind of nuclear power – the power that is produced when atoms come together to form larger atoms. This is the powerful energy source that makes the Sun shine and keeps us all alive. It also produces the terrible power of hydrogen bombs. It is called nuclear *fusion*.

In nuclear fission the atoms of heavy elements such as uranium and plutonium are split apart. In nuclear fusion, the atoms of light elements such as hydrogen and helium are forced together. Inside the Sun, it is the turning of hydrogen into helium that produces our light and heat.

Scientists have been trying for many years to make nuclear fusion work safely to produce all the energy we need. If they succeed, all our fuel shortages and power problems will end.

In a nuclear power station, the chain reaction is controlled. A nuclear reactor has rods containing some U-235 placed in a *moderator*. The moderator is usually graphite or water. In case the chain reaction starts to go too quickly, *control rods* are inserted too. These are made of metals that absorb neutrons and can be moved in or out of the reactor.

Heat is produced by the nuclear reaction and a cooling liquid or gas passes through the reactor to take up the heat. This coolant goes to a *heat exchanger* where it makes steam to drive steam turbines. These turbines make electricity.

Although the atmosphere stretches upwards from Earth for a few hundred kilometres, it is really a very thin shell compared to the size of the Earth. If the Earth were the size of an orange, the atmosphere would be no thicker than the skin. You can see this in the picture on the left.

# The Air We Breathe

Nothing can burn without oxygen. We can prove this by a simple experiment. Light a candle and stand it in a bowl of water. Place a jar over it. As the candle burns, the oxygen in the jar is used up and the water slowly rises inside the jar to take its place. Then the candle goes out. The oxygen has been used up.

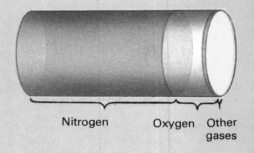

Nitrogen          Oxygen   Other gases

Our planet is surrounded by a blanket of air we call the *atmosphere*. It stretches upwards for several hundred kilometres and it contains gases that all living things must have. We are all in contact with air every second that we live, but we are seldom aware of it. It is quite invisible and has no taste or smell. You can feel the air when the wind blows. You can see clouds being pushed along by the air. Air can turn windmills. And if there were no air we would live in a silent world. Sound needs air to travel through. It cannot travel in a vacuum.

Although the atmosphere is hundreds of kilometres thick, over three-quarters of all our air is in the few kilometres nearest to Earth. As we go higher, the air grows thinner and thinner. At the top of a high mountain, there is so little air that we have difficulty breathing. There is not enough life-giving oxygen in each breath we take. That is why people who climb Mount Everest take their own oxygen supply with them. Inside airliners, the air pressure has to be kept as it is on Earth so that people can breathe normally.

Although we cannot see air, it is a substance just as rocks are. It is pulled down towards the Earth by the force of gravity – it has weight. When we talk about air pressure, we are talking about the weight of air pressing down on us, and air has quite a lot of weight. It presses on every square centimetre of our bodies with a force of over 1,000 grams.

In the experiment with the candle and the jar, it was found that extra water sucked into the jar was about one-fifth of the jar's volume. This shows that about one-fifth of the air is oxygen. Air is made up of a mixture of gases that we cannot see. Over three-quarters of it is nitrogen (78 per cent). As oxygen makes up about one-fifth (21 per cent), this leaves only 1 per cent, which is made up of small quantities of other gases such as *argon, helium, carbon dioxide, hydrogen, ozone,* etc. Air also contains some water vapour – separated particles of water too fine to see. When we talk about *humidity* we are talking about the amount of water vapour in the air. When the air holds as much water vapour as it can hold without mist appearing, we say the humidity is 100 per cent.

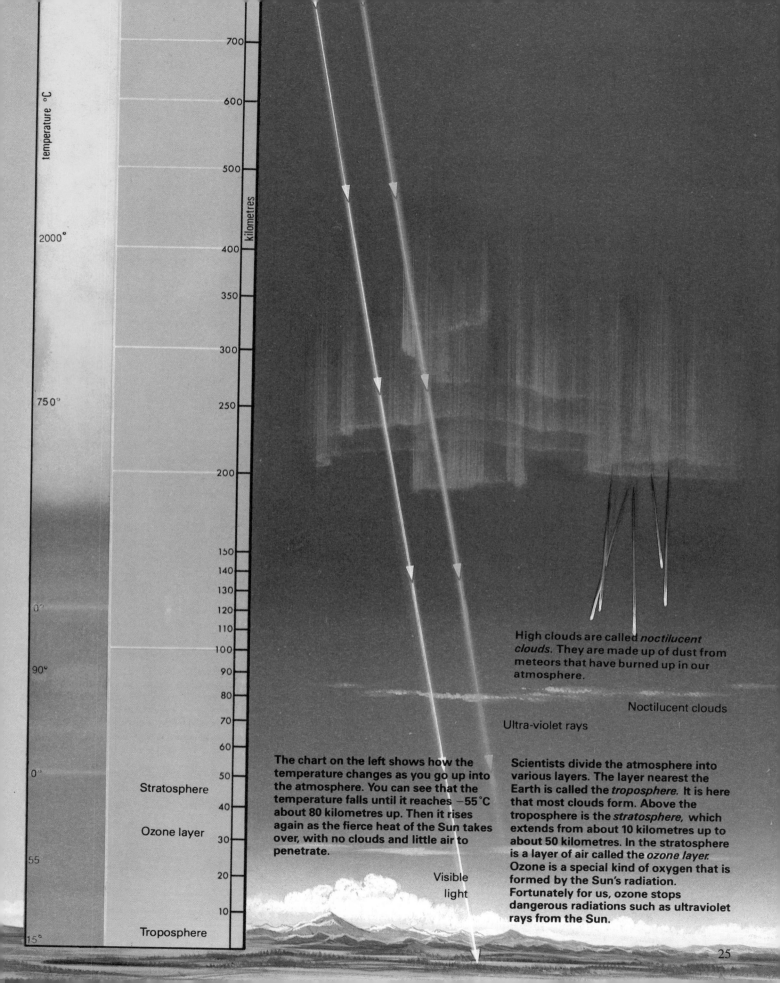

temperature °C

700

600

500

2000°

400

350

300

750°

250

200

kilometres

150
140
130
120
110

0°

100

90°

90

80

70

60

0°

50

Stratosphere

40

Ozone layer

30

55°

20

10

Troposphere

15°

High clouds are called *noctilucent clouds*. They are made up of dust from meteors that have burned up in our atmosphere.

Noctilucent clouds

Ultra-violet rays

The chart on the left shows how the temperature changes as you go up into the atmosphere. You can see that the temperature falls until it reaches −55°C about 80 kilometres up. Then it rises again as the fierce heat of the Sun takes over, with no clouds and little air to penetrate.

Scientists divide the atmosphere into various layers. The layer nearest the Earth is called the *troposphere*. It is here that most clouds form. Above the troposphere is the *stratosphere,* which extends from about 10 kilometres up to about 50 kilometres. In the stratosphere is a layer of air called the *ozone layer.* Ozone is a special kind of oxygen that is formed by the Sun's radiation. Fortunately for us, ozone stops dangerous radiations such as ultraviolet rays from the Sun.

Visible light

# The Body Machine

The human body is a wonderful machine. It is made up of millions upon millions of tiny cells which group together to form organs such as the heart and lungs. Inside a thin covering of skin and a framework of bones are all the different parts that allow us to move, breathe, speak and eat. Our eyes, ears and other senses tell the brain what is going on outside our bodies. The brain controls everything that we do.

We breathe in air so that our bodies can have a constant supply of oxygen. Without this gas, all our cells would quickly die. We eat to give our bodies fuel.

Our lungs are like a pair of bellows in our chest. We have a sheet of muscle called the *diaphragm* stretched across the bottom of our chest. When this and the rib muscles contract, the space in our chest grows bigger. Air rushes in through our nose and into our lungs. When air goes into our lungs, it passes through finer and finer tubes until it enters tiny air sacs called *alveoli*.

The alveoli are covered with a network of fine blood vessels. Oxygen passes from the air into the blood and the blood gives back carbon dioxide gas to the lungs. The blood carries oxygen to all parts of our bodies.

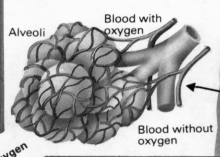

Air in

Carbon dioxide out

Blood with oxygen

Alveoli

Blood without oxygen

Lung

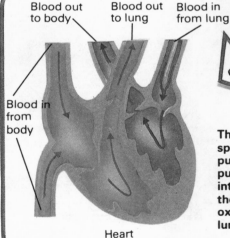

Blood out to body

Blood out to lung

Blood in from lung

Blood in from body

Oxygen

Heart

The heart is a pump, but a very special one. It has two separate pumping systems. The left side pumps oxygen-carrying blood into our *arteries* and all around the body. The right side pumps oxygen-free blood back to the lungs.

Food

Blood is red because it contains millions of tiny discs which we call the red blood cells. It is these cells that carry the oxygen around our bodies. Blood also contains white cells that help to defend the body against disease. The red and white cells float in a watery liquid called *plasma*.

Oxygen

Blood travels all over the body through a vast network of blood vessels. First of all it goes through our arteries. Then it travels through finer and finer tubes until it reaches very fine vessels called *capillaries*. The capillaries give food and oxygen from the blood to all the body's cells. In return, the cells give the capillaries carbon dioxide and other waste materials that travel back to the heart through our *veins*.

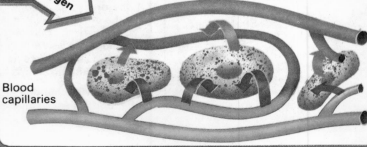

Blood capillaries

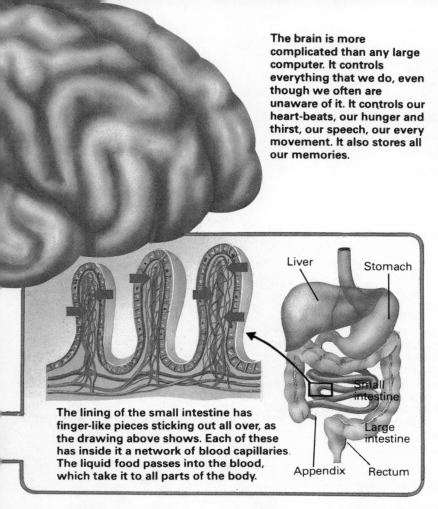

The brain is more complicated than any large computer. It controls everything that we do, even though we often are unaware of it. It controls our heart-beats, our hunger and thirst, our speech, our every movement. It also stores all our memories.

## The Nervous System

The nervous system controls all the other systems in our body. It has two main parts. The first part is made up of the brain and the spinal cord that runs down our back inside the backbone. The other part of the nervous system is made up of nerves that go out from the spinal cord and the brain to the various parts of the body.

The nerves are rather like telephone wires. When the doorbell rings, a message goes from our ears to our brain. The brain decides what we should do about it and sends messages to various parts of our body, telling them to work together and get out of our chair. Our muscles contract in the right order; we go to the door and open it.

## Reflex Actions

But not all our actions have to be ordered by the brain. If you touch a very hot plate, you pull your hand away instantly without having to think about it. This is called a *reflex action*. Nerves in our hand detect the heat and shoot a message to a nerve centre in the spinal cord. The nerve centre immediately sends back a message to the hand to draw itself away.

Liver

Stomach

Small intestine

Large intestine

Appendix

Rectum

The lining of the small intestine has finger-like pieces sticking out all over, as the drawing above shows. Each of these has inside it a network of blood capillaries. The liquid food passes into the blood, which take it to all parts of the body.

Our food stays in the *stomach* for some time. There it is squeezed and churned and mixed with juice. Then it passes slowly into the *small intestine,* a coiled tube about 6 metres long. Two glands, the *liver* and the *pancreas,* are connected to the small intestine. The liver pours a liquid called *bile* into the intestine. This helps to digest fat. The pancreas sends in substances called *enzymes* that also help to break down the food.

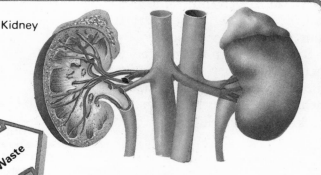

Kidney

Waste

The removal of waste from our bodies is called *excretion.* Several important organs work to get rid of waste. We lose water as sweat through our skin. We breathe out carbon dioxide and water from our lungs.

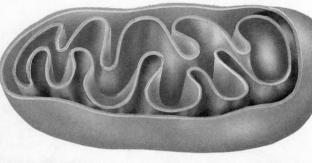

gen

The cells in our bodies have inside them hundreds of tiny sausage-shaped objects called *mitochondria.* (The one in the picture above is very much enlarged.) Mitochondria are power stations. They burn up the food we eat to give us energy. There may be as many as 800 of them in one tiny cell.

Energy

Our two *kidneys* (pictured above) get rid of most of our unwanted water and other waste. They filter our blood and we get rid of the waste as urine. The *liver* is the largest gland in our body. As our blood passes through the liver, its poisons and waste are removed. The liver also stores substances that our body uses when they are needed.

# Your Body

As you are looking at this book, reading the words and understanding them, your body is breathing, hearing, moving, feeling, digesting your last meal, making you hungry for the next, and performing hundreds more tasks without you even noticing. The different parts of the body do different jobs and each part depends on the others.

**Breathing in**

**Oxygen in**

**Breathing out**

**Carbon dioxide out**

**Lung**

**Diaphragm**

**Breathing**

We all need the gas oxygen to stay alive and we give our bodies a steady supply by breathing. When we breathe in our ribs move upwards, expanding the chest, and a flat muscle beneath the lungs moves downwards. This sucks air into our lungs, which fill up like two big balloons. Oxygen then passes through the thin walls of the lungs into the blood, and a waste gas, carbon dioxide, passes out of the blood to be exhaled when we breathe out.

## Bones and Bending

Your body gets its shape from its frame of bones – your skeleton. Without your skeleton you would be just a blob. The bones hold you up and enable you to move. There are lots of bones of different sizes and they meet at joints. Your elbow is a joint, so are your shoulders and your hips and your knees. Your elbow works like a hinge moving backwards and forwards. Your shoulder joint lets your arm move right round like a ball in a socket. Which way do your hips and knees work?

Bones do not move by themselves. They are moved by muscles which are attached to them. Muscles work in pairs, one working, one resting.

## Digesting our Food

A machine needs fuel to make its parts work. Our fuel is our food. When we swallow food it goes down a pipe to the stomach and mixes with chemicals which break it down into a liquid. This goes into the intestines, a coiled tube which churns up the liquid food until it is pure enough to go into our blood.

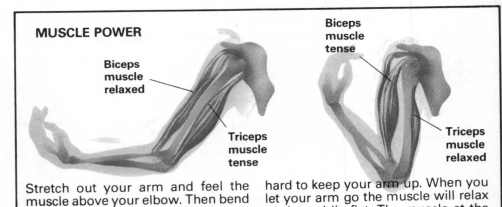

**MUSCLE POWER**

**Biceps muscle relaxed**

**Triceps muscle tense**

**Biceps muscle tense**

**Triceps muscle relaxed**

Stretch out your arm and feel the muscle above your elbow. Then bend your arm and feel how much shorter and harder the muscle is. It is pulling hard to keep your arm up. When you let your arm go the muscle will relax again and lie flat. The muscle at the back of your arm will then be tense.

## Skin Deep

On the outside of your body is your skin. It is not just a layer that keeps everything else inside, like a paper bag, it is alive and working, keeping you warm and dry and safe from harm. The tiny hairs in your skin keep you warm but if you get too hot your skin sweats. Water oozes from its surface and cools you down.

**Hair**

**Sweat gland**

**Oil gland**

**Hair follicle**

**Blood vessels**

**Fat**

**Muscle**

**Nerve**

Inside a tooth there are nerves and blood vessels. Each tooth is rooted firmly in the gum and has a hard surface. Teeth have to work very hard, biting and chewing all our food.

Enamel

Dentine

Root

Nerves and blood vessels

Retina

Optic nerve

Muscle

Iris

Lens

Pupil

Inner ear

Ear drum

Nerve

Outer ear

Bones

Cochlea

Liver

Stomach

Intestines

Wind pipe

Lungs

Heart

Arteries

Veins

Skeleton

## Sight and Sounds

You find out about what is going on outside your body through your senses. Your eyes work like cameras. Light from outside goes through a hole called the pupil, through a lens and forms an image on the inner surface of the eye. A nerve carries a message to the brain so that you know what you have seen.

Sounds coming into your ear hit your eardrum, just as a drumstick hits an ordinary drum. The movement of the eardrum sets off a chain of little bones that hit each other and carry the sound to a nerve. This nerve carries the message to the brain and you hear the sound.

## Your Brain

Without your brain you could not hear or see. You could not do anything, for the brain is in charge of everything. Even while you are asleep it is on duty, keeping you breathing and making sure that all the parts of the machine are working together. It is like a vast computer, so complicated that nobody has ever been clever enough to understand exactly how it works.

## Blood

Your blood is a great transport system, carrying food to all parts of your body, and removing any unwanted materials. Your heart acts as a pump to keep the blood circulating. It pumps blood through your arteries into tiny blood vessels, called capillaries, that reach right to your fingertips. Then the blood returns through the veins to your heart. As well as food, the blood also carries oxygen, which is needed by your body to make energy.

Apart from transporting materials through your body, your blood is also responsible for protecting you against infection and diseases, and keeping you healthy.

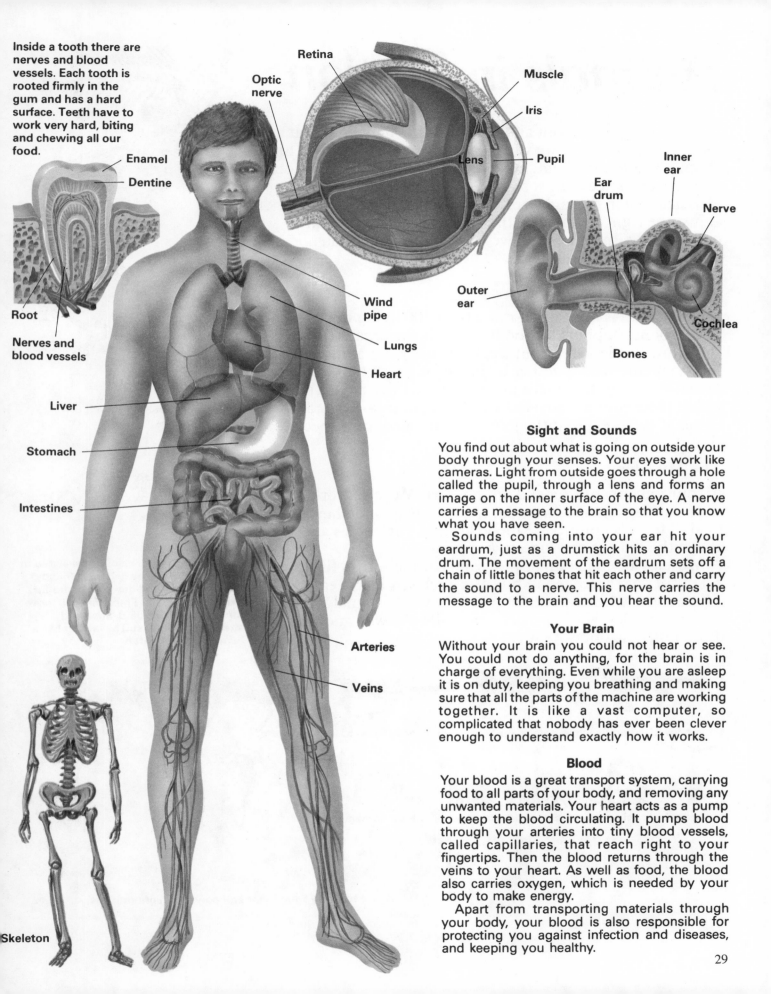

# Animals in Motion

If we had to think about all the things that happen to our bodies when we run, we would never be able to do it! Think about just a few of them. We bend and unbend joints in our feet, ankles, knees, hips, shoulders, elbows and wrists. Muscles pull in the right order to make all these joints work at just the right moment. Other muscles make us breathe more deeply. In fact, when we run we use more than a hundred different muscles.

## The Skeleton

Our skeleton is built up of more than 200 living bones. These bones support our body, protect the organs inside us, but allow us to move about freely. Bones meet at movable joints and are held together by bands of tough tissue called *ligaments*. To let the bones move smoothly against each other, their ends are covered with a pad of tissue called *cartilage* (gristle). And the joint is kept 'oiled' by a special liquid.

## The Muscles

All our movements depend on muscles. Muscles work our arms and legs, make us smile, turn our eyes and chew our food. They also pump the blood around our bodies and churn the food in our digestive system.

Muscles are made up of thousands of long, thin fibres. The fibres are arranged in bundles enclosed in a sheath. These muscle fibres contract when they get a signal from a nerve. Muscles work in pairs; one pulls one way and the other pulls the opposite way.

The skeletons of all animals are suited to their way of life. The fish has a 'bendy' backbone. The bird has light bones for flying. The dog has limbs that can move forward and backward, bend and straighten and twist. The lobster has a hard outside skeleton.

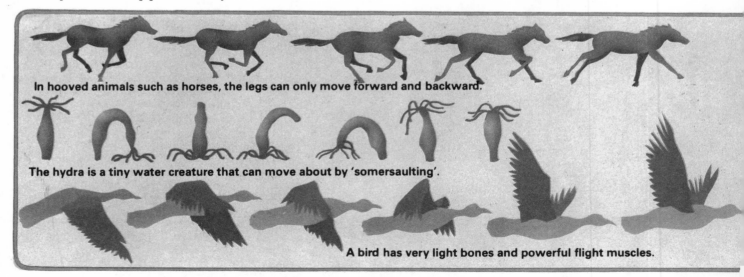

In hooved animals such as horses, the legs can only move forward and backward.

The hydra is a tiny water creature that can move about by 'somersaulting'.

A bird has very light bones and powerful flight muscles.

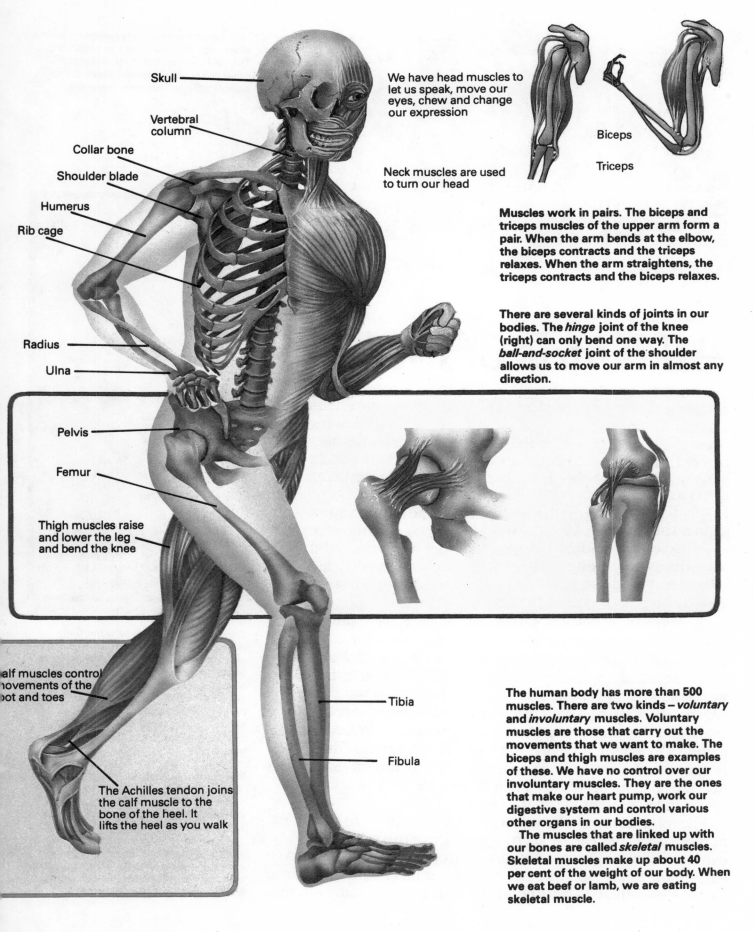

Skull

Vertebral column

Collar bone

Shoulder blade

Humerus

Rib cage

Radius

Ulna

Pelvis

Femur

Thigh muscles raise and lower the leg and bend the knee

...alf muscles control ...ovements of the ...oot and toes

The Achilles tendon joins the calf muscle to the bone of the heel. It lifts the heel as you walk

We have head muscles to let us speak, move our eyes, chew and change our expression

Neck muscles are used to turn our head

Biceps

Triceps

Muscles work in pairs. The biceps and triceps muscles of the upper arm form a pair. When the arm bends at the elbow, the biceps contracts and the triceps relaxes. When the arm straightens, the triceps contracts and the biceps relaxes.

There are several kinds of joints in our bodies. The *hinge* joint of the knee (right) can only bend one way. The *ball-and-socket* joint of the shoulder allows us to move our arm in almost any direction.

Tibia

Fibula

The human body has more than 500 muscles. There are two kinds – *voluntary* and *involuntary* muscles. Voluntary muscles are those that carry out the movements that we want to make. The biceps and thigh muscles are examples of these. We have no control over our involuntary muscles. They are the ones that make our heart pump, work our digestive system and control various other organs in our bodies.

The muscles that are linked up with our bones are called *skeletal* muscles. Skeletal muscles make up about 40 per cent of the weight of our body. When we eat beef or lamb, we are eating skeletal muscle.

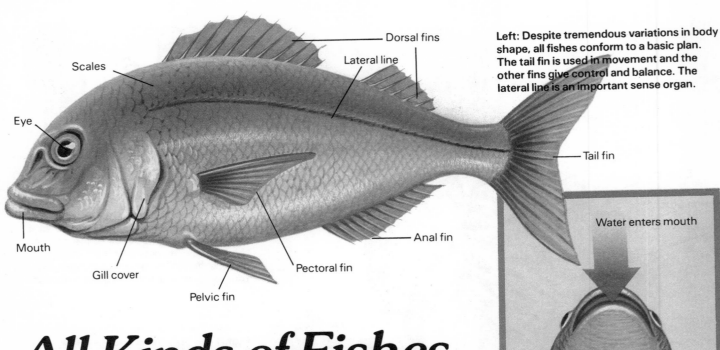

Scales — Dorsal fins — Lateral line

Eye

Mouth

Gill cover

Pelvic fin — Pectoral fin — Anal fin — Tail fin

**Left: Despite tremendous variations in body shape, all fishes conform to a basic plan. The tail fin is used in movement and the other fins give control and balance. The lateral line is an important sense organ.**

Water enters mouth

Water leaves via gill openings

# *All Kinds of Fishes*

The fishes are a very varied and successful group of vertebrate animals which have colonized the world's oceans, lakes and rivers. Fishes are cold-blooded creatures whose bodies are covered with scales. They are specially adapted to live and breathe in water, although some can spend limited amounts of time on dry land.

Among the most primitive of fishes are the lampreys and hagfishes. These eel-like creatures do not possess proper bones nor a proper set of jaws. Nevertheless, they are a successful group and have, instead of jaws, a rasping sucker. They feed by attaching themselves to the sides of other fishes and rasping away at their flesh.

Sharks, rays and skates lack proper bones as well, but they have a strong cartilage skeleton to support their bodies. Most sharks have a fearsome array of teeth in their powerful jaws. They are mainly predatory creatures which hunt other fishes as well as squid and various invertebrates. In tropical waters there are species of shark which reach huge sizes. Both the feared tiger shark and the man-eating great white shark often exceed 6 metres in length. The massive whale shark, on the other hand, is harmless to man, feeding on microscopic plankton. Skates and rays are relatives of sharks. Their bodies are flattened, for they spend much of their life on the seabed.

The most numerous group of fishes are the bony fishes. Most of those which we eat, or keep as pets, are in this group. The extraordinary lungfishes are found in tropical lakes. They survive the dry season by curling up in a mud chamber. Their 'lung' allows them to breathe air through a small opening in the chamber.

**Above: Fishes breathe by extracting dissolved oxygen from the water, using a series of internal gills over which water is continually passed. The process can easily be observed in aquarium fishes and first involves the fish taking in water through the mouth. With the mouth closed, a swallowing movement forces the water over the gills and out through the gill openings.**

**Right: The pike is often called the freshwater shark, because of its voracious appetite and its fearsome array of teeth. It takes its prey by surprise and its body is well adapted for this purpose. The markings on its flanks provide camouflage as it lurks in the weeds, and its large tail fin gives it excellent acceleration. With its huge gape it can easily grab prey and the teeth prevent its escape.**

# Other Bony Fishes

The cod family are large, bony marine fishes which provide food for man as well as many other fishes and birds. They usually have large eyes and mouths, and powerful bodies which enable them to swim well. Some of them can live in very deep water. The herring family are also important for food, and are found in vast shoals in some seas where many birds and other creatures depend on them for food. The salmon family are streamlined and powerful swimmers, and many of them live in the sea, but make long migrations up rivers to spawn.

In fresh water, members of the carp family are very common, ranging in size from tiny minnows to the large carp themselves, and they include the familiar goldfish.

Tropical lakes and rivers support large numbers of fishes from the cichlid family which are often brightly coloured and very active swimmers.

The perch family are armed with spines and strong scales and hunt other fishes for their food.

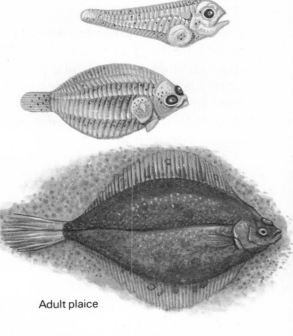

Adult plaice

Female

Nest

Male

Above: When the young plaice hatches from its egg it is much like any other bony fish. After a few days, however, changes begin to take place and one eye moves across the top of its head. Eventually it ends up alongside the other and the young fish begins to swim on one side with its eyes uppermost. It is now perfectly adapted to life on the sea bottom.

Far left: In the spring the male stickleback builds a little nest into which he lures a female. If satisfied with the arrangements, she lays her eggs in the nest and departs. For a couple of weeks, the male guards the eggs and looks after the young when they hatch, herding them back into the nest at the first sign of danger.

Above left: The mouthbrooder protects its eggs in a most unusual way. After they have been fertilized, the female collects the eggs in her mouth and carries them around until they hatch.

33

# The Insect World

Insects are found everywhere except in the open sea and the frozen Poles. There are more different species of insects than all the other animals put together. About a million have been identified, and more are being found all the time. They vary in size from fairy-flies just 0.2 millimetres long to stick insects 330 millimetres long and bulky Goliath beetles which weigh 100 grams.

Insects can always find somewhere to live and something to eat. Insects live in ponds and streams, in caves, up mountains and in deserts. Almost every kind of plant and animal substance has an insect that feeds on it. Insects play an important part in disposing of dead plants and animals, so that the substances of which these are made are returned to the soil to feed new plants. Many insects are essential for plants, anyway, because they pollinate them. They transfer pollen from one flower to another so that seeds will form from which new plants can grow.

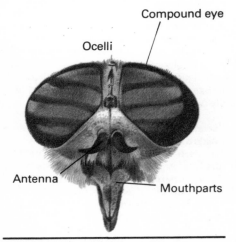

Compound eye

Ocelli

Antenna

Mouthparts

## SEEING ALL AROUND

Insects cannot move their eyes to see around them. But to make up for this most species have two large *compound eyes*. Each compound eye has from 6 to 30,000 tiny lenses, depending on the species, and each lens is set at a slightly different angle. This gives the insect a wide field of vision. In addition many adult insects also have three simple eyes, called *ocelli*. The simple eyes can only detect light and dark. A typical insect's head, above, shows the two kinds of eyes, and also the antennae, or feelers, and the mouthparts, for chewing or sucking.

## All Kinds of Insects

Entomologists – people who study insects – group the million or so different species into 29 main orders, according to the classification described on page 22. These orders are listed at the top of the facing page. So little is known about some of these orders that the insects in them have no common name, only a Latin one.

Although insects vary so much in shape and size, they all have the

Some of the many different shapes and kinds of insects are shown opposite. Honeybees, right, spend their lives collecting pollen and nectar from flowers. A worker bee lives for only about six weeks.

**Above:** Ants foraging for food lay down a scent trail. This enables them to find their way back to the nest, and also guides other ants to the source of food. Like bees, wasps and termites, ants are social insects, with three castes: queen, males, and workers, who are female.

Honeybees

# THE 29 DIFFERENT GROUPS OF INSECTS

**WINGLESS INSECTS**
Silverfish (Thysanura)
Two-pronged bristletails (Diplura)
Protura (tiny soil dwellers with
   no common name)
Springtails (Collembola)

**INSECTS WITH WINGS**
**A: With three-stage metamorphosis**
Mayflies (Ephemeroptera)
Dragonflies (Odonata)
Stoneflies (Plecoptera)
Grylloblattodea (soil-dwellers
   with no common name)
Grasshoppers (Orthoptera)
Stick insects (Phasmida)
Earwigs (Dermaptera)
Web-spinners (Embioptera)
Cockroaches (Dictyoptera)

Termites (Isoptera)
Zoraptera (tropical insects with
   no common name)
Booklice (Psocoptera)
Biting lice (Mallophaga)
Sucking lice (Anoplura)
True bugs (Hemiptera)
Thrips (Thysanoptera)
**B: With four-stage metamorphosis**
Lacewings (Neuroptera)
Scorpionflies (Mecoptera)
Butterflies, moths (Lepidoptera)
Caddis flies (Trichoptera)
True flies (Diptera)
Fleas (Siphonaptera)
Bees, wasps, ants (Hymenoptera)
Beetles (Coleoptera)
Twisted-wing parasites
   (Strepsiptera)

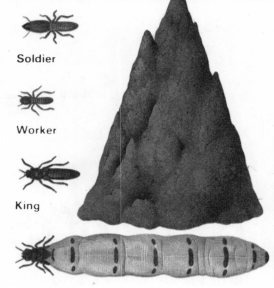

Soldier

Worker

King

Queen

**Termites have a more elaborate caste system than ants, and build more elaborate nests – some termite mounds are 6 metres (20 feet) or more high. The termite castes are queen; king, who lives with her; workers, male and female, and soldiers. Queens and kings live a very long time, anything from 15 to 100 years.**

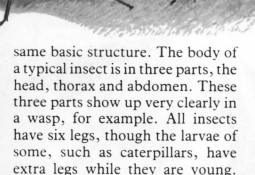

same basic structure. The body of a typical insect is in three parts, the head, thorax and abdomen. These three parts show up very clearly in a wasp, for example. All insects have six legs, though the larvae of some, such as caterpillars, have extra legs while they are young. Nearly all adult insects have wings, and can fly.

Insect ways of life vary enormously. Mayflies, dragonflies and caddis flies are among those which spend most of their lives in the water, emerging for just a brief life in the air as adults. Ants, bees, wasps and termites are social insects, living in big, well-organised colonies, and working together.

Many insects are parasites, living on other animals. The best known are fleas and lice, but there are also many kinds of tiny parasitic wasps. Aphids and other true bugs suck the juices from plants. Most insects lay their eggs and forget about them, but some, such as bees and earwigs, look after their young.

Small copper butterfly

Bumblebee

Ant

Stag beetle

Lacewing

Meadow grasshopper

Bluebottle

Flea

Leafhopper

Gull

Hawk

Goose

Pigeon

Cormorant

Tern

Buzzard

# Birds of the Air

Birds are animals with wings and feathers. Most of them can fly, and to make this possible their bones are very light and very strong. There are about 9,000 different species. The most familiar are the perching birds, which have claws that grasp twigs and branches. They include all the garden songbirds. Birds with webbed feet for swimming spend their lives in or near water. Birds of prey hunt other birds and small mammals. Birds such as the kiwi cannot fly.

Above: Birds in flight can often be identified by their outlines, seen against the sky. Some typical outlines are shown here. Small animals learn to recognise birds of prey and quickly seek shelter from their sharp talons.

Below: Birds' feet are shaped to suit the kind of life they lead – climbing, perching, swimming or running.

Below: The talons of a golden eagle are shaped for seizing prey such as this young rabbit, which is just able to reach the safety of its hole.

Swimming (Mallard)

Running (Partridge)

Perching (Greenfinch)

Climbing (Woodpecker)

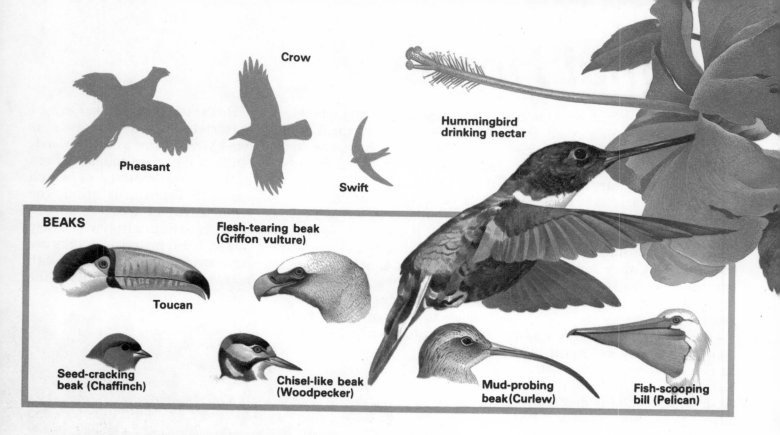

Crow

Pheasant

Swift

Hummingbird
drinking nectar

**BEAKS**

Flesh-tearing beak
(Griffon vulture)

Toucan

Seed-cracking
beak (Chaffinch)

Chisel-like beak
(Woodpecker)

Mud-probing
beak (Curlew)

Fish-scooping
bill (Pelican)

**Above: Beaks are shaped to deal with the different kinds of food. The short, stout beak of the chaffinch, for example, is ideal for eating seeds. And the long beak of a hummingbird is adapted to probing deep into flowers for nectar. But the value of its huge, gaily-coloured beak to the fruit-eating toucan is unknown.**

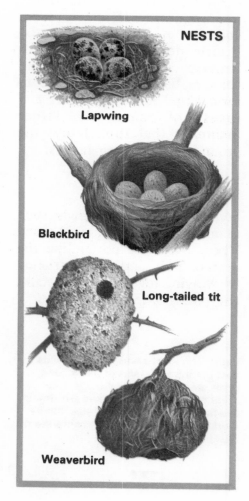

**NESTS**

Lapwing

Blackbird

Long-tailed tit

Weaverbird

Birds range in size from the ostrich, which is up to 2.45 m tall and weighs 155 kg, to the bee humming-bird, only 50 mm long including the tail, and weighing less than 3 g.

As a rule, male birds are more brightly coloured than the females, and they use their smart feathers to help them when courting. One reason for the duller colours of females is that it helps them to be less conspicuous when sitting on the nest hatching their eggs, and so less likely to fall victim to predators.

Although all birds have some kind of voice, only about a third of them are real singers. Ornithologists – people who study birds – are not really sure why birds sing: some appear to sing in order to warn off rivals, others sing to attract mates. But some do seem to sing just for pleasure.

Birds have very varied diets. Some feed mostly on seeds, and have strong beaks to break open the seed cases. The finches are examples of seed-eaters. Birds such as thrushes feed on insects and worms, and many birds have a mixed diet of insects and seeds.

The seabirds, such as gulls, catch fish, using their long bills to seize them. Hawks and other birds of prey feed on small animals. Birds such as vultures eat carrion, the dead bodies of animals.

Birds have many ways of flying. The broad wings of eagles and hawks enable them to soar and hover in the sky, looking for prey. The long narrow wings of swallows give them great speed, which they need because they catch insects in the air. The even longer wings of the albatross enable it to stay airborne at sea for days at a time.

# Animal Homes

Animals such as antelopes, bison and elephants which roam the wide plains do not have a settled home. Birds and many insects construct temporary homes in which to lay their eggs and rear their young. Some animals build permanent homes for themselves, often with great skill. This skill is not something they learn, but is born in them, and is part of that mysterious quality known as instinct.

Only a few mammals build homes, and they are mostly the smaller creatures, which construct burrows underground. Often these underground homes are for more than one family. For example, marmots, living mostly in mountain districts, form colonies of 10 to 15 animals. Prairie dogs, found in North America, have similar-sized colonies, but link them together to form large 'towns'. Badgers and foxes are among the larger mammals that tunnel into the ground to make their homes.

## The Nest Builders
Some other small mammals, such as mice and squirrels, build nests. These nests are not unlike the nests of birds, and are constructed by weaving together twigs, stalks and pieces of leaves.

**Right: The tiny harvest mouse builds its nest among the stalks of reeds, long grass, or growing cereal crops. Like other rodents, its front paws are almost like hands, which greatly helps it in its work. A harvest mouse can complete its nest in less than 10 hours.**

The best-known home builders are birds. Most of them build afresh every year, but some, such as the white stork of Europe, merely clean up and repair the same nests year after year.

Nest-building techniques vary a great deal. Birds whose young are born with feathers and can leave the nest almost at once make very simple nests. Swans and ducks do this. Most chicks, however, are helpless to begin with and need a warm, secure place to grow up in.

Birds use a great variety of materials, often whatever is handy. A sparrow in Switzerland, home of the watch industry, even built a nest entirely of watch springs! Tailorbirds stitch the large leaves of trees or shrubs together to form a bag, which they line with soft materials. Storks use large twigs, often reinforced with rags, straw and mud. Mud is the

Harvest mice are among the smallest mice in the world: a single specimen weighs 9 grams; its length is 200 millimetres. Half of this is the tail, used to help in climbing.

main material used by swallows, swifts and martins. Woodpeckers, with their chisel-like beaks, make holes in tree-trunks.

A few fishes, such as salmon and sticklebacks, build nests to lay their eggs in, but the jawfishes build actual homes: deep wells lined with pebbles, where they lie in wait for their prey.

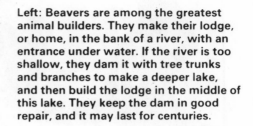

Left: Beavers are among the greatest animal builders. They make their lodge, or home, in the bank of a river, with an entrance under water. If the river is too shallow, they dam it with tree trunks and branches to make a deeper lake, and then build the lodge in the middle of this lake. They keep the dam in good repair, and it may last for centuries.

Below: Termites are the most skilled insect builders. Some species build mounds as much as 7 metres high, and they equip them with ventilating shafts. They also bore wells to get water.

1    2    3    4

Left: Badgers generally make their home, called a set, in or on the edge of a wood. A well-established badger set can be up to 5 metres deep, and cover an area 30 metres across. A large set of this kind has many rooms and passages, with several entrances, and is usually home for more than one family.
Badgers are very clean animals; from time to time they take their bedding out and air it, and they dig their latrines at a little distance from the set. Sometimes foxes move into part of a badger set, but the badgers then wall off the foxes' home to keep out the smell.

Above: There are many species of weaverbirds, but the work of the village weaver of East Africa is a typical example:
1  The male bird selects a forked twig of a tree and starts to twist strips of leaf round it. He uses blades of grass or strips torn off palm leaves.
2  Gradually the nest starts to take shape.
3  The bird knots strands on to the twig, or on to other strands, and weaves them in and out as if using a loom.
4  The finished nest has a long flight tube as an entrance.

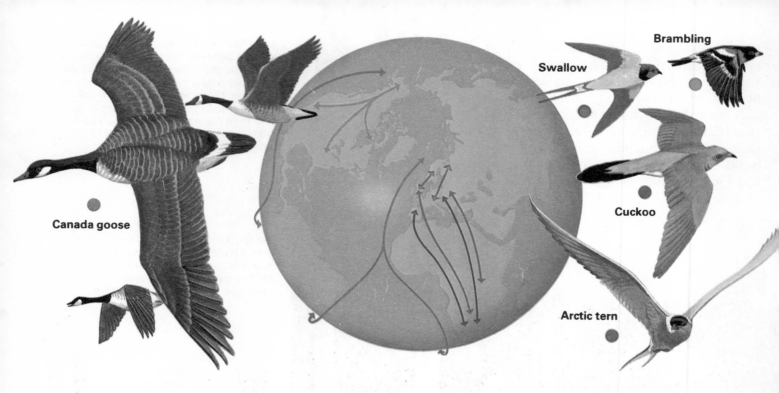

Canada goose

Swallow

Brambling

Cuckoo

Arctic tern

# Animal Journeys

In search of food, or a place to breed and rear their young, many animals make long journeys each year. This annual travelling is called *migration*.

Birds are the best known migrants. Many spend the summer months in cooler lands and fly to warmer places for the winter. Swallows, for instance, arrive in Europe in late spring. They build their nests, rear their young, and feast upon insects. Then, as the autumn days grow shorter, they leave in great flocks. Guided only by instinct they fly south to Africa.

Other animals that migrate include many fishes, whales and seals, some insects, especially butterflies, and the large grazing animals such as deer and antelope.

**Above:** Some of the routes taken by migrating birds. The Arctic tern flies from the Arctic to the Antarctic and back in search of perpetual summer.

**Below left:** Seals migrate to their breeding grounds in spring, then return to warmer seas in winter.
**Below centre:** Salmon spend most of their lives at sea, but return to the rivers where they were born to breed their own young.
**Below right:** Sea turtles come to land in the same places every year to lay their eggs.

## Navigation

Sailors and airmen use a great variety of aids to navigate across the world – compasses, maps, charts, radar, and chronometers for keeping accurate time. But birds have travelled for millions of years without any of these things to guide them.

After experimenting with starlings and homing pigeons, scientists came to the conclusion that they and many other birds navigate by means of the Sun and the stars. Other experiments suggest that birds can detect the magnetic field of the Earth, just as a compass needle does.

Right: The Monarch butterfly of North America makes one of the longest migrations undertaken by any insect. In summer these butterflies are found in North America as far north as the shores of Hudson Bay. Their young migrate south to Florida and Mexico, where they hibernate on trees. In spring they fly back to the north.

Below: The Sargasso Sea is a region of the western Atlantic Ocean that is full of densely floating seaweed. In these quiet waters baby eels hatch from their eggs. At this stage they look like tiny willow leaves. They drift slowly east across the Atlantic, growing until they turn into elvers, the next stage of development. They travel up rivers and turn into adult eels. After several years they return to the Sargasso to lay their eggs and die.

Below: The musk ox is a strange animal, midway between a sheep and an ox. Musk oxen roam in herds, feeding on grass in the river valleys of north-east Canada and Greenland in the summer, and migrating to higher ground in winter. There, the wind blows much of the snow away so they can get at the vegetation beneath. The animals form a tight circle when wolves threaten them.

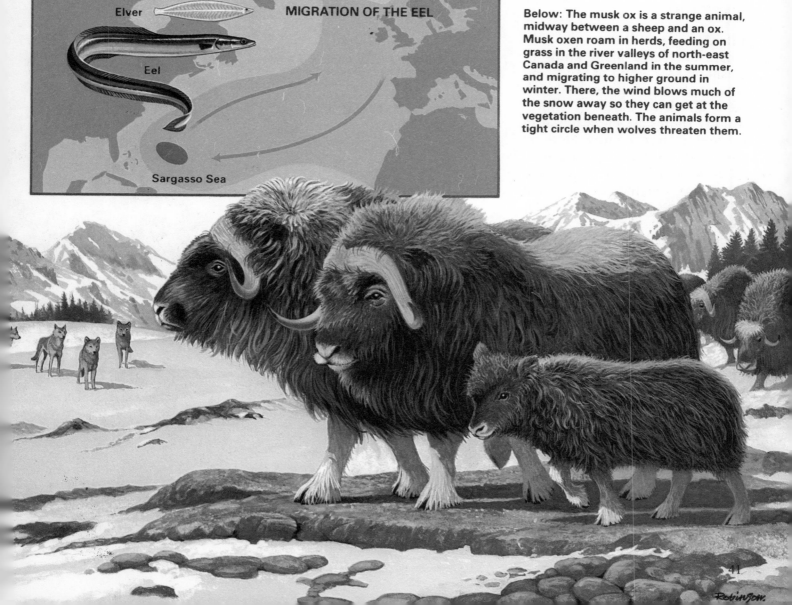

Elver

MIGRATION OF THE EEL

Eel

Sargasso Sea

# The Seashore

The seashore is a place of violent contrasts. Plants and animals living there are under water for part of the time, and exposed to air, with possibly fierce winds or sizzling sunshine, the rest of the time. They may also be battered by heavy waves.

Over millions of years, living things on the shore have adapted to these harsh conditions. The only plants that can survive on the shore are seaweeds. Seaweeds are a form of algae, simple plants related to the green scum often seen on ponds. Although some appear to have stems and leaves, these features are merely divisions of the main body.

The shore-living animals have various methods of defence against waves and sunshine. Some burrow deep into the sand or mud. Others have hard shells, and cling to rocks. Soft-bodied animals such as sea anemones shelter in clefts under rocks.

## Life Along the Shore

There are three main kinds of seashore: rock, sand or mud, and shingle. Some stretches of beach have all three kinds of shore. Muddy shores are often found in or close to river mouths. Nothing can live on shingle beaches, because when the waves crash on shore they roll the stones to and fro, grinding everything up. For this reason, it is rare to find an unbroken shell on shingle.

Rocky shores are the home of seaweeds, which are not found on sand or mud. There are three main kinds of seaweed: green, brown and red. The colours vary, and some browns are a greenish shade, while many reds look brown. Small animals take shelter under seaweed from the drying effect of sun and wind.

Molluscs, related to garden snails and slugs, are among the main animals on rocky shores. Some, such as sea snails and limpets, have only one shell. Others, such as mussels, have a pair of shells, called valves, hinged together.

## THE THREAT TO THE BEACHES

The biggest threat to life on the seashore is not the heat of the Sun, the drying wind, or the blows of the waves, but pollution made by Man. Every year tons of debris are washed on shore, especially near busy sea lanes such as the English Channel. This includes old plastic containers and other waste matter thrown overboard from passing ships. Sometimes deck cargo is carried away in a storm, and this can include drums of poisonous or otherwise harmful chemicals.

An even bigger threat is posed by oil, spilled from ships, and especially from wrecked tankers. The oil coats all animals with which it comes in contact, and kills them.

From the land, sewage is pumped into the sea, and sometimes the tides bring it back on to the shore.

Fortunately, countries are now passing laws to try to keep the sea, and the shore, clean.

Below: Some of the many animals to be found in and around a rock pool. There are several different kinds of seaweed: bladderwrack has little bubbles of air along its fronds, which help it to float.

Cormorant

Limpet

Dog-whelk

Common starfish

Sea anemone

Hermit crab

Rock goby

Sea anemone

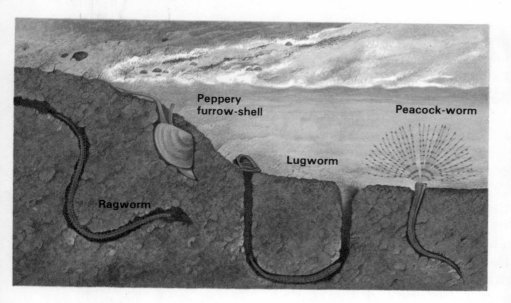

Peppery furrow-shell

Peacock-worm

Lugworm

Ragworm

Left: When the tide is in on a sandy beach, animals such as the peacock-worm come out of their burrows and open up. But, when the tide is out, they and the other burrowers stay firmly underground.

Below: Some of the many shells to be found on the beach. Some, such as the scallop, swim freely in the water near the shore, and live specimens are rarely washed up or left at low tide.

Queen scallop

Keyhole limpet

Grooved razor shell

Edible cockle

Edible periwinkle

Pelican's-foot shell

Tower shell

Thin tellin

Common whelk

Many rocks are thickly covered in barnacles. They are related to crabs, which are also found on rocky shores, and on sand, too. There are often pools among the rocks, which never dry out. All these animals live in rock pools, along with soft-bodied creatures such as sea anemones.

More molluscs live on sandy shores, but they burrow deep into the sand and are not easy to find. They include tellins, razorshells, carpetshells and cockles. Also hidden under the sand are many kinds of worms, including lugworms, ragworms and peacock-worms.

Bladderwrack

Barnacles

Topshell

Mussels

Sea urchin

Shore crab

# Cold Lands

The polar regions are the coldest and bleakest places on Earth. Antarctica, around the South Pole, is mostly covered by thick ice, and fierce blizzards blow loose snow over the surface. Temperatures rarely rise above freezing point during the day and a world record −88.3°C has been recorded near the South Pole. No people live permanently in Antarctica, but some scientists work there in heated homes under the ice. Penguins live around the shores of Antarctica and the seas are rich in fish and whales.

Polar bears live on the ice floes of the Arctic Ocean, hunting seals and young walruses. And around the Arctic Ocean are parts of North America, Europe and Asia, called the *tundra*. Here the snow melts during the short summers, when temperatures may rise to 10°C. Flowering plants then carpet the ground, but it is too cold for trees. Migrating animals such as reindeer graze in the tundra. Arctic people include the Eskimos. They once lived by hunting. They built winter homes of ice called igloos, but most Eskimos now have modern homes.

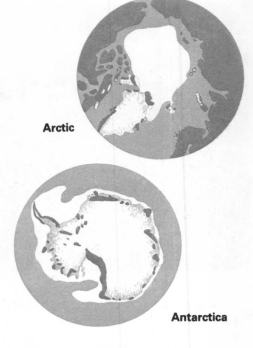

Arctic

Antarctica

Above: One map shows the ice-covered continent of Antarctica around the South Pole. The other map shows the region around the North Pole, which contains the icy Arctic Ocean. The northern parts of North America, Europe and Asia surround this ocean. These lands have long, cold winters, but plants grow in the short summers.

Below: Penguins gather in large colonies on the icy coasts of Antarctica. The emperor penguin hatches its egg on its feet and the young birds huddle together for warmth.

Most people in the great Sahara Desert live around oases. These fertile places have wells or springs which tap water in rocks below the surface. Some nomads cross hot deserts in camel caravans. Camels are called the 'ships of the desert'. This is because they can go long distances without drinking. But when they reach an oasis, they often drink up to 100 litres of water in only 10 minutes. The camel is suited to the desert in another way. A web of strong skin connects its two widely spaced toes and prevents its feet from sinking into the sand.

Many animals live in the desert despite the heat and the dryness. The smaller animals hide away during the day to escape the fierce sun and venture out at night. Many of them get the water they need from the seeds they eat.

# Hot Deserts

Hot deserts cover about one-fifth of the world's land areas. They have mostly clear skies and high temperatures. The average rainfall is under 250 millimetres a year. Several years may pass with hardly any rain, then a thunderstorm may drench the land. Seeds which have been dormant for years rapidly germinate and many plants flower. When this happens in the Australian desert, people flock to the area to see this superb spectacle.

The world's largest desert is the Sahara in North Africa. It contains sand dunes, plains of loose gravel and bare, rocky uplands. Most plants in hot deserts, such as thorn bushes and cacti, are drought-resistant. The most useful desert animal is the camel. It can go for long periods without water. It loses weight, but regains it when it drinks. Deserts become fertile when they are irrigated (watered). Some deserts, like those of the Middle East, are rich in oil and natural gas. These fuels lie hidden far below the surface.

Penguins are awkward creatures on land, waddling around on their webbed feet. To move faster they slide on their bellies over the ice, pushing themselves along with their stubby wings. In the water penguins are fast and agile as they chase fish under water.

# Grasslands

Tropical grasslands, called savanna, campos or llanos, occur north and south of the equator in Africa, South America, southern Asia and northern Australia. They are in warm regions with high rainfall. But, because they have a marked dry season, forests do not develop except in such areas as river valleys. Tropical grasslands are used for cattle rearing and some crop farming. But there is a danger that the winds will blow away the exposed soil in the dry season. Such soil erosion can make a region infertile in a few years. In Africa, the savanna supports many animals.

Temperate or mid-latitude grasslands have less rain and much colder winters than tropical grasslands. Trees are also rare on the dry, windswept plains. Huge areas of temperate grasslands, which are also called prairies, steppes or pampas, have become cattle ranches or vast wheat farms. The wildlife has been much reduced. In Australia, sheep have replaced most of the kangaroos and wallabies of the grasslands.

Above: Cattle ranching is a major activity in such savanna regions as East Africa.

Below: Temperate grasslands in North America have become leading wheat-growing regions. The land is flat and easy to farm.

# Woods and Meadows

Moist temperate regions have some rain all the year round, with warm summers and fairly cold winters. Such regions once had huge forests of deciduous trees, such as ash, beech, chestnut, hickory, maple and oak. These trees shed their leaves in winter in order to protect themselves against the cold. Such forests once grew over most of western Europe, northern China and the eastern USA, areas which now contain some of the world's most densely populated regions. Most of these forests have been cut down. Their wood was used for building and as a fuel. In the USA, the forests largely vanished in about 300 years and the land was used for farming. The wildlife dwindled and soil erosion became a serious problem. This also happened on the lower slopes of the mountains of South Island, New Zealand. Britain's forests were replaced by a pleasant landscape of ploughed fields, river meadows, hedgerows and occasional clumps of woodland. But the destruction of forests led to a great decline in wildlife.

Above: Forests once covered the moist temperate regions in the middle latitudes. In England, these forests have been replaced by a complicated patchwork of fields.

Below: Moist temperate regions in New Zealand support great numbers of sheep.

# Northern Forests

Cold snowy climates are warmer than polar regions, but colder than temperate regions. Vast coniferous forests, called taiga, grow in cold snowy climates. Coniferous trees include birch, fir, pine and spruce. These cold forests are found only in the Northern Hemisphere. No large land masses in a similar latitude exist in the Southern Hemisphere.

Many furred animals, such as ermine, mink, otter and wolverine live in the forests. They have attracted hunters, who have greatly reduced the numbers of these animals. Larger animals include bears, bull moose, caribou, reindeer and wolves. Many trees in these cold forests are valuable softwoods. They are cut down and floated along rivers to sawmills. Sawn timber is used to make furniture and many other things. Many logs are made into wood pulp and paper. The northern forests do not contain many people, because of the cold weather and their generally infertile soils.

**Above: The map shows the vast belt of cold coniferous forest that sprawls over North America, northern Europe and northern Asia. It lies south of the tundra and north of the deciduous forests and grassland.**

# Rain Forests

Rain forests grow in the tropics. Near the equator, there are areas which are hot and wet throughout the year. These regions support tall evergreen trees, such as ebony, mahogany and teak. The leaves of the trees block out sunlight from the muddy forest floor, so that few plants can grow there. The largest equatorial forests are in the Amazon basin of South America and the Zaire (or Congo) basin of Africa. Most wild animals live in the trees. Most people live in forest clearings. They grow food crops such as cassava, manioc and sweet potatoes. Large plantations produce cocoa, coffee, palm-oil, rubber and sugar-cane.

There are similar tropical forests in the monsoon lands of southern Asia and north-eastern Australia, where there is a dry season. But these forests are often less dense than equatorial forests. They also contain some trees that shed their leaves before the dry season in order to conserve water. Rice is the main food crop in monsoon lands. Equatorial and tropical forests are now being rapidly cut down.

Above: The map shows the world's rain forests, which grow in warm tropical regions. Below: The world's largest rain forest is in South America, in the Amazon River basin. It contains many animals, such as monkeys and colourful birds.

49

# River Valleys

Rivers carry worn pieces of rock from their upper courses to the sea. As the rocks move along, they break down into smaller and smaller pieces. Finally, they become fine alluvium. This alluvium is spread over river valleys when rivers flood. It sometimes piles up in deltas, areas of new fertile land at the river mouths.

Fertile river valleys and deltas are the most densely populated regions on Earth. Farmers can produce large crops because of the rich soil and plentiful water. Some valleys have been centres of early civilizations. These include the valleys of the Tigris-Euphrates in Iraq, the Nile in Egypt, the Indus in Pakistan, the Ganges in India, and the various river valleys of eastern China.

Above: Rivers flow swiftly down their steep upper courses but they become slow-moving when they near the sea. The lower valleys and deltas of many rivers are thickly populated. In parts of China, including Hong Kong, people live on river boats called sampans, right.

Below: Buffalo plough the flooded 'paddy' fields in which rice is grown. Rice from the great river valleys is the staple diet of Asia.

# Among the Mountains

Mountain regions are often remote, cold places, which are so difficult to climb and cross that they were once hide-outs for bandits. But they are also among the world's most beautiful places. They have varied scenery, because the higher one goes, the colder it gets. Temperatures fall by an average of 6.5°C for every 1,000 metres. High mountains near the equator have bands of vegetation ranging from rain forest at the bottom to polar climates on the ice-covered peaks.

Farmers often use high mountain pastures for summer grazing. For example, Swiss farmers live in sheltered mountain valleys in winter. In summer, they take their herds up to the high mountain slopes. To survive in mountains, animals must be able to move quickly over jagged slopes. One such animal is North America's bighorn, which is wonderfully sure-footed.

**Below: The sure-footed bighorn is at home among the steepest crags of the Rocky Mountains.**

**Cattle graze on the flower-strewn Alpine meadows.**

# The World of Plants

Without plants there would be no other life on Earth. For only plants can make their own food using simple materials – carbon dioxide gas from the air and water and mineral salts from the ground. Animals cannot make their own food: they feed either upon plants or upon each other. Plants also provide shade and shelter: birds, insects and mammals make their homes in trees.

There are about 500,000 species of plants, and they are classified in a similar way to animals. Many species of plants share the same common names.

**The Plant Kingdom**

There are several groups of simple plants: algae, which include seaweeds and the scum on ponds; fungi, such as toadstools; liverworts, and mosses. Then come the fern-type plants: ferns, clubmosses, and horsetails.

The next group of plants is called the *gymnosperms*, which means 'naked seeds'. They have their egg cells and pollen in cones, and include cycads, ginkgoes, and the familiar conifers. Finally come the flowering plants, known as the *angiosperms*, which means 'seeds in a case'.

All plants except the simplest work in the same way. A typical plant has a system of roots, which anchor it in the soil and also absorb water and minerals from the soil. The stem carries the water from the roots to the leaves. It also supports the leaves and raises them up to catch the light.

Trees, bushes and shrubs have woody stems. The wood in the middle of a tree trunk is very hard and no longer carries water, but it provides a strong support for the tree. The trunk grows a little thicker every year and you can tell the age of a tree stump by counting the number of growth rings across its trunk.

Right: The ripened seeds of flowering plants need to be widely scattered if the new plants are to spread and survive. Birds eat many of the juicy fruits, and the hard seeds pass through them and are scattered that way. Pods of peas and beans burst when they are ripe, hurling their seeds a considerable distance. Very light seeds such as those of dandelions and grasses are carried by the wind, and so are the heavier winged seeds of the sycamore.

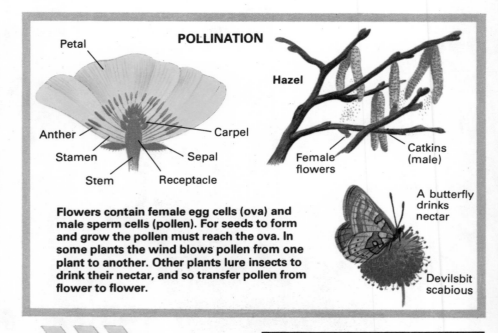

**POLLINATION**

Petal
Anther
Stamen
Stem
Carpel
Sepal
Receptacle

Hazel

Female flowers
Catkins (male)

A butterfly drinks nectar

Devilsbit scabious

Flowers contain female egg cells (ova) and male sperm cells (pollen). For seeds to form and grow the pollen must reach the ova. In some plants the wind blows pollen from one plant to another. Other plants lure insects to drink their nectar, and so transfer pollen from flower to flower.

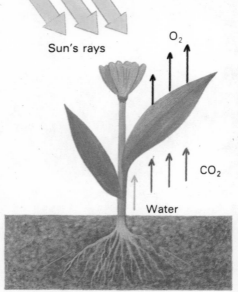

Sun's rays
$O_2$
$CO_2$
Water

## PHOTOSYNTHESIS

The process by which plants make their food is *photosynthesis,* which means 'building with light'. Most of the work is done by the leaves. They contain a green colouring substance called chlorophyll, which absorbs some of the light falling on the leaves and uses it as a source of energy for chemical changes. The leaves absorb carbon dioxide ($CO_2$) from the air, and water from the roots. They turn this $CO_2$ and water into sugar, which in turn can be turned into other substances to build up the plant's structure. The plant cannot use all the oxygen in carbon dioxide, and gives it off as oxygen gas ($O_2$). All animals need oxygen to live, and plants keep up the supply.

Thrush eating
hawthorn berry

Parachute-like
seed of dandelion

Wind blowing
grass seeds

## GERMINATION

1    2    3    4

When a seed falls on soil and the
weather is warm enough – as in
spring – it begins to germinate, that
is, to grow. The seed absorbs water
and swells, the case bursts open,
and a root appears, followed by the
first shoot.
Germination can be studied by
putting a bean in a jar lined with

blotting paper and keeping the
paper moist (1). Soon the young
root bursts from the seed (2) and
always grows downwards (3).
Finally the shoot springs up (4) and
the first leaves are formed. Once
this happens the plant can begin to
make its own food and grow
rapidly.

Goldfinch eating
plantain seeds

Dandelion
'clock'
shedding
seeds

Thistle
seedling

Thistles

Winged seeds
of sycamore

Poppy seeds
falling from
a seed pod

Dormouse nibbling
hawthorn berry

Ant carrying
poppy seed

# The Ocean Deeps

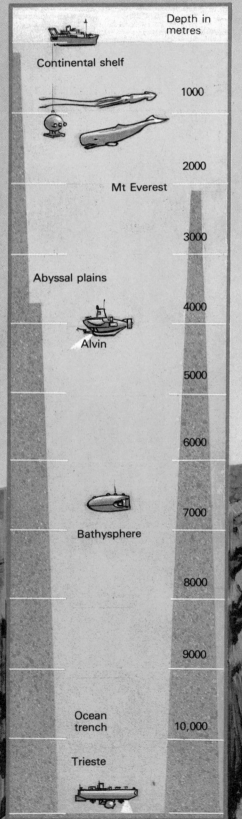

Depth in metres

Continental shelf

1000

2000

Mt Everest

3000

Abyssal plains

4000

Alvin

5000

6000

7000

Bathysphere

8000

9000

Ocean trench          10,000

Trieste

There are four principal oceans. The largest is the Pacific Ocean which covers about 165,724,000 km$^2$. This is about one third of the Earth's surface. The other oceans, in order of size, are the Atlantic, Indian and Arctic oceans.

## Continental Shelves

Around land masses are gently sloping areas covered by shallow seas. These areas are called continental shelves. In places, such as western South America, the continental shelf is narrow. But off Land's End, England, the continental shelf extends 320 kilometres to the west. Continental shelves are flooded parts of the continents. They end at the steep continental slopes which plunge down to the abyss, the deep part of the ocean. The tops of the continental slopes are the true edges of the continents.

**Left: If Mount Everest were placed in the deepest ocean trench, its peak would be about 2100 metres below sea-level. The diagram also shows the depths reached by various manned submersibles.**

## The Abyss

The abyss was once thought to be a mostly flat plain covered by oozes. But mapping has shown that it contains several striking features.

The ocean trenches are the deepest parts of the oceans. The Mariana Trench reaches a depth of 11,033 metres. The trenches are places where one plate is descending under another. As it descends, it melts. As a result, volcanic islands are found alongside the trenches. They get magma from the melting plates.

The ocean ridges are huge, long mountain ranges. Here, plates are moving apart and new crustal rock is being formed. Some volcanoes rise from the ocean ridges. Other volcanoes develop above isolated 'hot spots' in the Earth's mantle. Some volcanoes reach the surface as islands.

The largest ocean, the Pacific, is larger than all the continents combined. This view of the Pacific is called the water hemisphere.

Below: The diagram shows the main features of the oceans: the shallow continental shelves; the steep continental slopes; ocean trenches; volcanic mountains and islands; and long oceanic ridges.

# Continents Adrift

Only about a quarter of the surface of our planet is dry land. The rest is sea. Most of the Earth's land lies north of the equator and is broken up into the masses we call 'continents'. But it was not always so. Over 200 million years ago, when the first dinosaurs were beginning to roam the world, all the Earth's land was joined together in one huge mass. This great land mass has been called Pangaea. Over millions of years, Pangaea moved and broke up to form the continents as we know them. This movement is still going on at a rate that varies between a centimetre and 12 centimetres a year. It is called the 'continental drift'.

If we compare the shapes of the coasts of western Africa and eastern South America we can see that they fit together quite well. And if these continents are matched, not on the shore lines but at their under-sea *continental shelves*, the jigsaw fit is better still. (All the continents have under-sea shelves sloping out from them.) America and Africa were once joined together.

Lava

Magma

The picture on the left shows what happens inside a volcano. The deeper you go under the Earth's surface, the hotter it gets. At a depth of about 30 kilometres it begins to get so hot that some rocks simply melt. This molten rock is called *magma*. Some of this magma is pushed up through cracks and holes. These are volcanoes. There are different kinds of volcanoes. Some erupt quietly, oozing out molten rock called *lava*. The lava may spread out for kilometres before it cools and hardens. Lava of this kind builds gradually sloping mountains. Explosive volcanoes throw out rocks mixed with gas and steam that has been trapped underground.

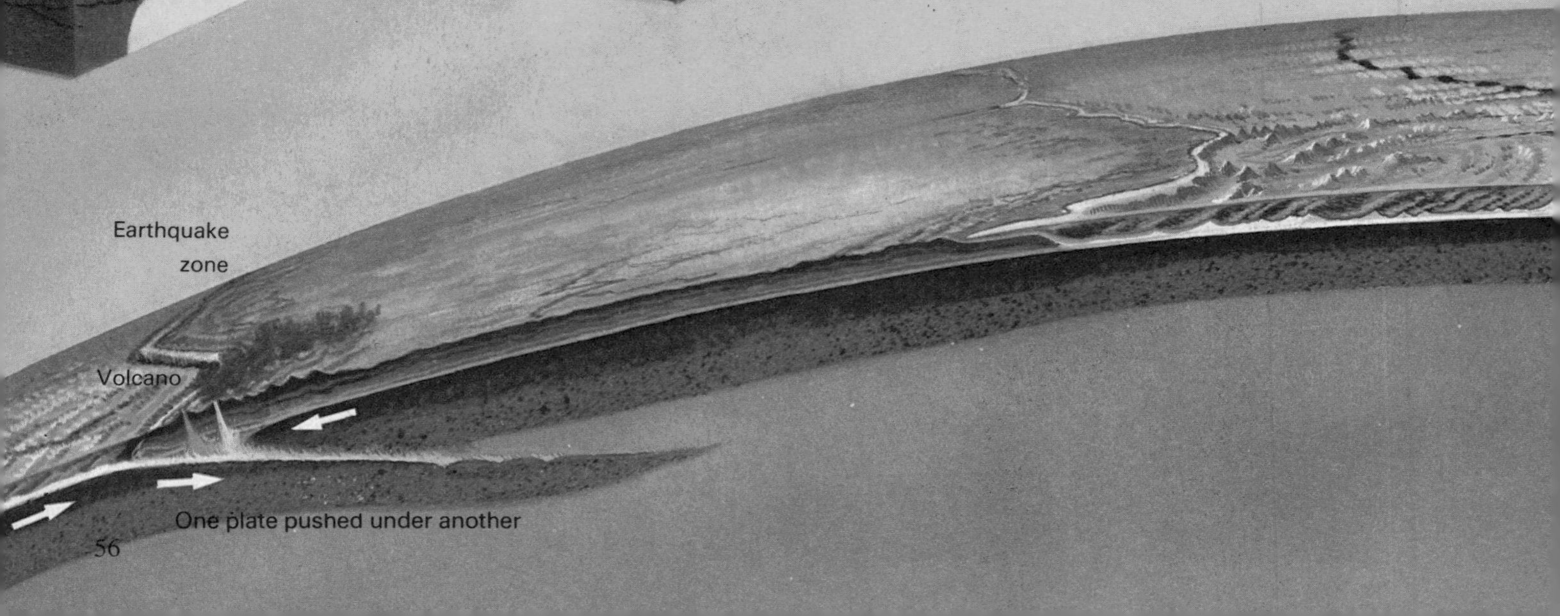

Earthquake zone

Volcano

One plate pushed under another

The Earth's crust beneath our feet is made up of two main kinds of rock. Great blocks of granite-type rock, which we call the continents, are embedded in a heavier kind of hot, half-liquid rock. The continents are great plates 'floating' on the hot rock underneath. They move very slowly, but the huge mass of the plates means that they move with tremendous force. When two plates come towards each other, the great force of the meeting pushes one plate under the other. In plate collisions such as this, mountain ranges are slowly pushed up and there may be earthquakes.

In the course of time, the continents have travelled enormous distances. By examining fossils in the rocks, and by other means, scientists are able to plot the history of a place's climate. They know, for instance, that frozen Antarctica was at one time in the tropics. And it is possible to tell the likely future movements of the continents. Africa, for example, will drift north, slowly closing the Mediterranean Sea. Australia will continue its slow journey northward. And by measuring magnetic field directions fixed in rocks of different ages, experts have been able to plot the drift of Britain's North Sea oil rocks from the time when they were south of the equator 400 million years ago.

The theory of the drifting continents has also helped to explain how closely related animals are found in lands now separated by thousands of miles of sea.

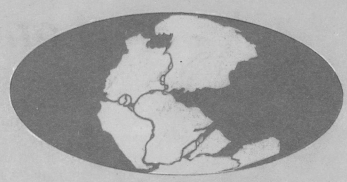

200 million years ago

60 million years ago

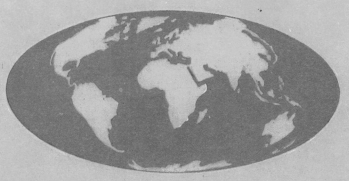

Today

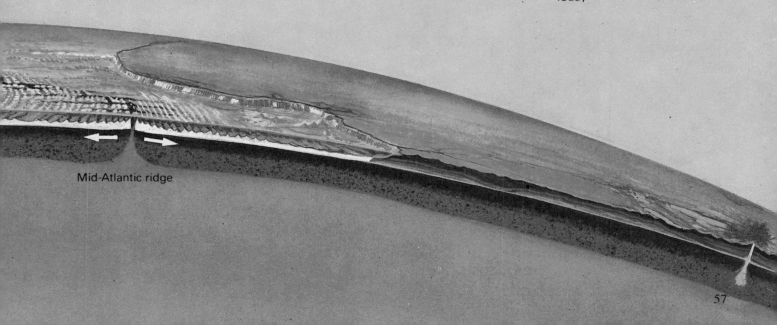

Mid-Atlantic ridge

# Landscapes

The surface of the Earth and the landscapes we see around us are slowly changing all the time. Rain, sun, wind and frost constantly break down rocks. Great mountain ranges are worn down to rolling plains in millions of years. Solid rock is ground into mud. We call this breaking up and wearing away *erosion*.

Running water is the most important force in changing the land. Rain washes soil down hillsides and sinks into the ground, to appear elsewhere as streams and rivers. The rivers cut into their banks and beds and carry stones and mud down to the sea. Sometimes streams travel underground and hollow out caves.

Erosion is at work in deserts, too. There the wind piles up loose sand in huge, shifting dunes. Wind-blown sand blasts exposed rocks, polishing and carving them into strange shapes.

But erosion does more than just alter the landscape. It makes soil. Soil is just surface rock that has been broken down and mixed with decayed plants.

Some of the strangest effects of erosion can be seen in deserts, where sharp grains of sand are blown by the wind. The sand is blasted against fixed rocks, smoothing them into fantastic shapes.

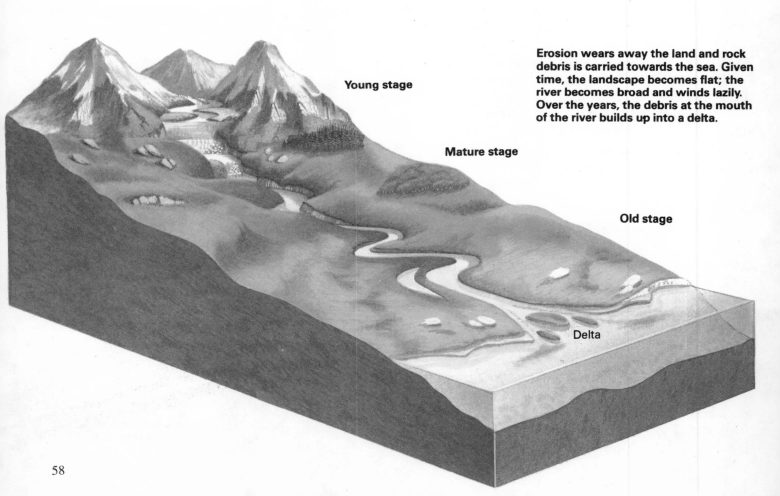

Young stage

Mature stage

Old stage

Erosion wears away the land and rock debris is carried towards the sea. Given time, the landscape becomes flat; the river becomes broad and winds lazily. Over the years, the debris at the mouth of the river builds up into a delta.

Delta

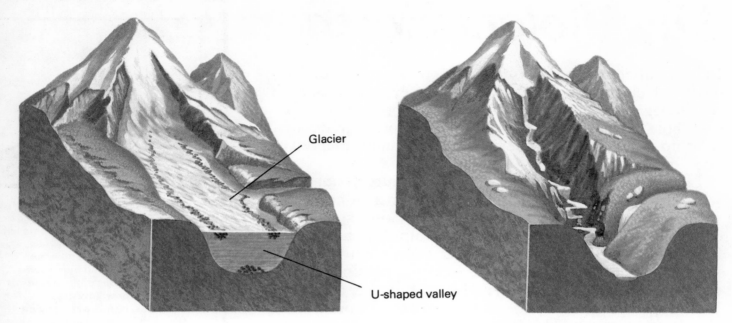

Glacier

U-shaped valley

## Frost Shattering

In cold places, ice is important in shaping the landscape. Water running down the mountain slopes seeps into cracks in the rock. As the water freezes, it expands with enough force to split the rocks apart. (The same thing happens when water freezes in our house pipes and bursts them.) Millions of tons of frost-worn rock litter mountain slopes.

## Rivers of Ice

High in the mountains, snowfalls build up into solid ice, sometimes hundreds of metres thick. These are glaciers, great rivers of ice which slowly make their way down a valley at a rate of about a metre a day. Glaciers are very powerful. As they move along, they pick up boulders and debris and carve away the valley floor and sides.

After the Ice Ages, the land had been changed by glaciers. Great U-shaped valleys had been formed. Vast areas of land were covered with boulders, sand and clay that had been moved about by the rivers of ice.

## The Sea Versus the Land

Another form of erosion is by the sea. Around our coasts, the sea is constantly eating away at the land. In some places it cuts steep rock cliffs. In others it carries sand and pebbles along the coast to dump them on gently sloping shores. So are born sand and pebble beaches. Sometimes the sand is dumped at the entrance to a bay, where it gradually forms a bar or spit which may cut the bay off from the sea.

**During the Ice Ages, rocks, firmly embedded in the glacier, turned the glacier into a giant 'file' which wore down the surrounding rocks into a deep valley.**

**When the Ice Ages passed, the glacier was replaced by a mountain river.**

**Pounding waves wear away the land into steep cliffs.**

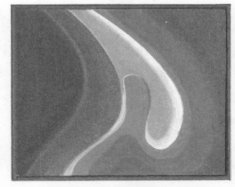

**Sandy beaches are built up from tiny fragments worn away from cliffs and rocky coasts.**

# The Violent Earth

In November 1963 a new island rose out of the sea off the coast of Iceland. This island, called Sertsey, is a volcano which began life on the ocean floor. Lava poured out of a *vent* (hole) in the Earth's crust and, as it cooled, gradually built up to form the massive cone which finally emerged as an island.

Lava comes from huge pockets of molten rock (magma) which form far below the surface of the Earth. When volcanoes erupt they are said to be *active*. Some spout columns of black ash high into the air; others pour blazing lava down their slopes in great streams. People living on the slopes must abandon their homes as fast as possible before they are buried under hot ash and lava. But after a volcano has stopped erupting and becomes *dormant* (sleeping), the people often return. This is because lava and ash make rich soils which are good for farming.

## Earthquakes

Earthquakes are caused by many things, including volcanic eruptions. But most occur when rocks move against each other along great cracks in the Earth's crust. One such fault in California, the San Andreas Fault, is 960 km long. In 1906 it caused a devastating earthquake when the rocks along its length slipped by over 6 m. The buildings in San Francisco swayed and collapsed, and fires soon raged through the city. In October 1989 another earthquake in San Francisco measured 5.7 on the Richter scale. Many people died when a flyover collapsed onto their cars, but more buildings remained standing than in 1906, as architects had learnt to build 'earthquake proof' buildings.

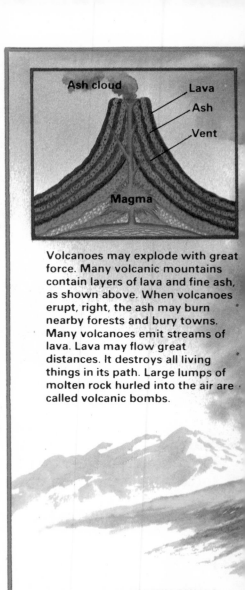

Volcanoes may explode with great force. Many volcanic mountains contain layers of lava and fine ash, as shown above. When volcanoes erupt, right, the ash may burn nearby forests and bury towns. Many volcanoes emit streams of lava. Lava may flow great distances. It destroys all living things in its path. Large lumps of molten rock hurled into the air are called volcanic bombs.

Volcanic ash

Lava

Volcanic bombs

Tornadoes are destructive storms. They are whirlwinds and are common in the south-central United States. They are only about 440 yards across, but they can lift people and animals into the air and make buildings collapse. In 1925 a tornado in the USA killed 689 people in only three hours.

Earthquakes on the ocean floor cause disturbances in the water which can create huge waves. Known as tidal waves, or *tsunamis* (the Japanese name), they crash over nearby coasts and cause great havoc.

## Tornadoes and Hurricanes

Fierce storms can also be devastating. One violent storm is a whirlwind called a tornado. Tornadoes are small in size, but fast winds in the center of the tornado leave a trail of destruction. Other large storms are called hurricanes, typhoons or tropical cyclones. They form over the oceans and move towards the land. Howling winds drive waves on to the land which, combined with heavy rain, flood coastal areas, drowning people and animals.

# Sun, Wind and Rain

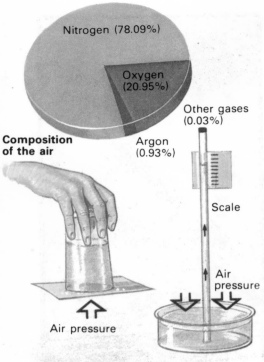

Nitrogen (78.09%)

Oxygen (20.95%)

Other gases (0.03%)

Argon (0.93%)

**Composition of the air**

Scale

Air pressure

Air pressure

Air is invisible, but we can weigh it in a laboratory. This is done by weighing an open jar and then weighing it again after we have pumped out the air. The difference between the measurements is the weight of the air in the jar. Roughly, the air in a drinking glass weighs about the same as an aspirin tablet.

The belt of air around the Earth is called the atmosphere. More than 99 per cent of the air is within 40 km of the surface. The chief gases in the air are nitrogen and oxygen. There are small amounts of carbon dioxide, which plants absorb, and tiny amounts of ozone. Ozone is important because it blocks out most of the Sun's harmful ultraviolet rays. The air also contains invisible water vapour formed when the Sun's heat evaporates water from the Earth.

The atmosphere is always moving. At the equator, the Sun's rays heat the air, which causes it to rise. This creates a

**Top: Diagram to show the various amounts of gases in the air. Above: A simple barometer, a device used to measure air pressure. Air presses down on water in a basin which forces water up the tube. As the air pressure changes, so the level of the water moves up or down against the scale. Above left: To illustrate the effect of air pressure, put a card over a glass of water and upend the glass. Air pressure will hold the card in place and stop the water escaping.**

**Below: The water cycle provides the land with a regular supply of fresh water. The Sun evaporates water from the oceans. This condenses into clouds which bring rain to the land. Rivers carry the water back to the oceans.**

**VARIOUS CLOUD TYPES**

Cirrus

Cirrostratus

Cirrocumulus

Altostratus

Altocumulus

Stratocumulus

Cumulonimbus

Cumulus

Stratus

Nimbostratus

Precipitation: the water falls from the clouds to the land as rain

The water vapour condenses to form clouds

Transpiration: water is given off by trees and other plants

Evaporation from lakes and rivers

Water seeps into the ground and flows downhill towards the sea

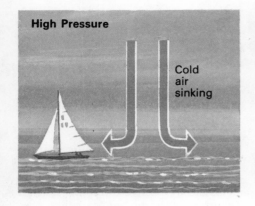

**High Pressure**

Cold air sinking

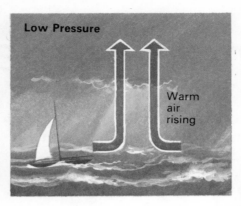

**Low Pressure**

Warm air rising

**Snowflakes**

zone of low air pressure, called the *doldrums*. The rising air eventually cools and spreads out north and south. It sinks back to Earth in the *horse latitudes* (around 30° north and 30° south). Because the air is sinking, these are zones of high air pressure. From these zones, some air flows back to the equator in the trade winds, and some flows polewards as the westerly winds.

The westerly winds meet up with cold easterly winds blowing from the poles. Depressions, which bring changeable, rainy weather, form in areas where the warm and cold air meet. Rain forms when air cools and water vapour condenses (liquefies) into tiny droplets. In temperate regions, extremely cold water droplets in clouds freeze around ice crystals. Finally, heavy crystals fall and melt to become raindrops. But if the air is cold, they fall as snow.

**Left:** On sunny days, the Sun heats the surface of the Earth, which warms up the lower layers of air. The warm air rises, carrying with it much invisible water vapour. As the air rises, it cools. Cool air cannot hold as much water vapour as warm air, and so some water vapour condenses into visible water droplets or ice crystals. These particles are so small that they stay suspended in the air and form clouds. If the upward air currents are strong, the clouds grow in size into huge cumulonimbus, or thunderstorm, clouds. In these clouds, the droplets and crystals collide and grow in size. When they are heavy enough, they fall as raindrops. But if the air near the ground is cold, they fall as snowflakes (above).

In regions where the air is sinking, far left, the air pressure is high. This happens in the horse latitudes, where the air gets warmer as it descends. Regions of high air pressure are associated with fine, stable weather and cloudless skies.

**Right:** At the equator the Sun's rays heat a far smaller area than at the poles, where the rays hit the Earth's surface at an angle. For this reason the heating is greatest at the equator. Here, the hot air rises and spreads out north and south, sinking back to Earth around the horse latitudes. At the surface, some air flows back towards the equator in the trade winds; some flows polewards in the westerly winds. Cold easterly winds blow from the poles.

The Sun's heat causes water to evaporate from the oceans

Water flows into the sea by land and river to complete the cycle

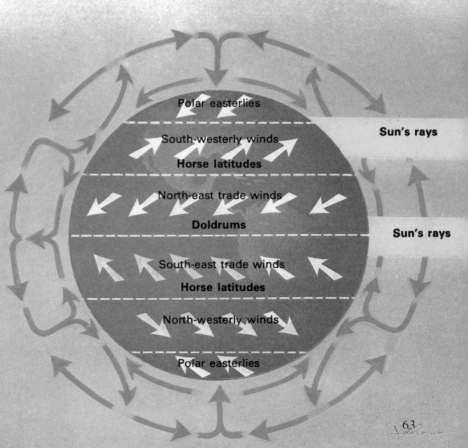

Polar easterlies
South-westerly winds
**Horse latitudes**
North-east trade winds
**Doldrums**
South-east trade winds
**Horse latitudes**
North-westerly winds
Polar easterlies

**Sun's rays**

**Sun's rays**

# Storm and Tempest

About 45,000 thunderstorms occur every day around the world. They form when warm air rises rapidly, creating towering cumulonimbus clouds.

Some thunderstorms occur along cold fronts in the depressions that bring stormy weather to temperate regions. Others occur in tropical areas. Here, the Sun heats the surface in the morning and strong currents of air sweep water vapour upwards. Huge cumulonimbus clouds with anvil-shaped tops form and raindrops start to fall in the late afternoon. Following a storm, the sky clears in the early evening.

Less common, but more dangerous, storms are hurricanes, which occur north and south of the doldrums. Hurricanes have caused millions of dollars' worth of damage in the south-eastern USA. The USA is also hit by whirlwinds, or tornadoes. A tornado in 1925 killed 689 people in the south-central USA in three hours.

## HURRICANES

Because of their size and high wind speeds, which reach 300 km/h, hurricanes are the most destructive storms. They form over the oceans a little way north and south of the equator. They are also called tropical cyclones, typhoons or willy-willies.

When these storms approach land, they cause floods. About 11 strike the coasts of North America every year. They are tracked by the Hurricane Warning Service at Miami, Florida. The meteorologists use satellite photographs and reports from ships and aircraft in order to discover in which direction and at what speed the hurricanes are moving.

**Below: The diagram shows a depression moving from left to right. High cirrus clouds appear ahead of the warm front. Medium and low clouds follow and rain falls. Thunderstorms are features of the cold front.**

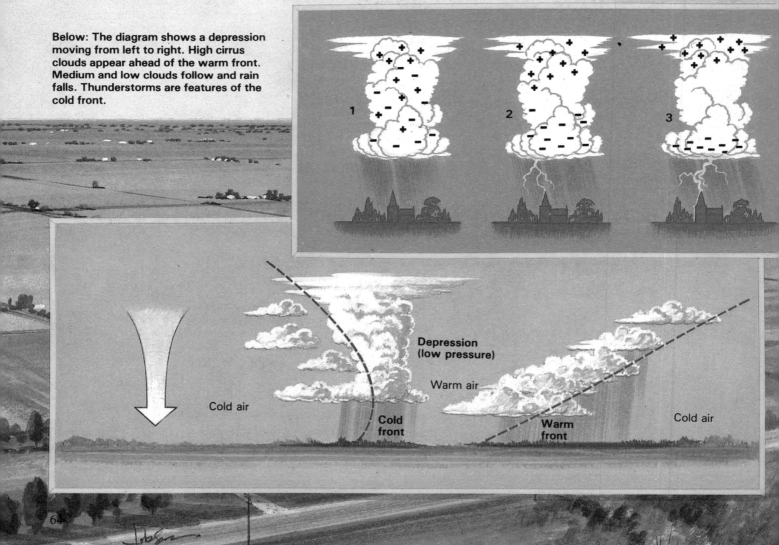

Depression (low pressure)

Warm air

Cold air

Cold front

Warm front

Cold air

**Right:** Tornadoes are small but destructive storms. About 500 to 600 hit the mid-western USA every year. They form when a funnel-like column of air sinks down from a thundercloud. Warm air rises and swirls around this column. At ground level, tornadoes are only about 0.4 km across. But wind speeds may reach 650 km/h and people may be lifted into the air.

**Left:** Lightning occurs in cumulonimbus clouds, because positive electrical charges build up in the tops of clouds and negative charges at the bottom (1). When the charges have separated, the electricity is often discharged in a probe stroke (2) and a bright return flash (3). Lightning also leaps from the base of clouds to the positively charged ground. Thunder is caused by the intense heat along the channel followed by the lightning. We see lightning before we hear thunder, because light reaches us faster than sound.

# Tomorrow's Weather

Ships' navigators and airline pilots depend for their safety on weather forecasts, while farmers need them so that they can protect their crops. Also millions of ordinary people plan tomorrow's activities only after they have checked the local weather forecast.

## Weather Stations

Meteorologists at weather stations on land and at sea collect information about the weather every few hours. They use thermometers to measure temperatures, barometers to measure the air pressure and hygrometers to measure the humidity (moistness) of the air. They also record wind speeds and directions, rainfall amounts, hours of sunshine, cloud types and the visibility. Radiosondes send back readings of the temperature, pressure and humidity at various levels in the upper air (see the diagram on the facing page).

Weather satellites provide pictures of the cloud patterns on Earth, while radar networks show areas where rain or snow is falling. All the information obtained at weather stations is sent, in code, to weather forecasting centres.

| Weather symbols | | Wind speed (in knots) | |
|---|---|---|---|
| Mist | ⚌ | Calm | ◎ |
| Fog | ☰ | 1-2 | |
| Drizzle | , | 13-17 | |
| Rain | ● | 48-52 | |
| Sleet | ✹ | Cloud cover (in eighths) | |
| Snow | ✳ | None | ○ |
| Shower | ▽ | 1 or less | ◐ |
| Hail | △ | 4 | ◕ |
| Thunder | ⌐ | Total | ⊗ |
| Haze | ∞ | Warm front | |
| Smoke haze | ∿ | Cold front | |
| Squall | ⋁ | Stationary front | |
| | | Occluded front | |

# Preparing Weather Forecasts

At weather centres, the information from many weather stations is fed into a computer. The computer produces weather charts which show weather conditions at various levels of the atmosphere. These charts cover extremely large areas. Meteorologists study these charts and find out how the weather has been changing in recent hours. This gives them a good idea of how the weather will change over the next 12 to 24 hours. They summarize their ideas on *prognostic* (forecast) charts. Written forecasts for particular areas are then prepared from the charts. These are sent to newspapers and radio and television stations.

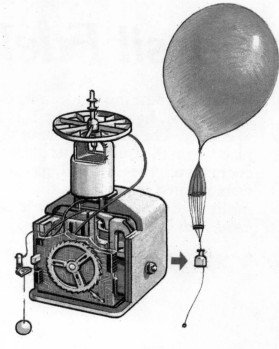

**Opposite:** Weather satellites circle the Earth taking regular photographs of the changing cloud patterns and collecting information about the upper air.

**Below:** Weather charts, like topographic maps, use many symbols which indicate weather conditions at various places. The numbered lines, resembling contours, are isobars. Isobars join places with the same air pressure. The fronts are zones of unsettled weather.

**Right:** Instruments used to measure weather conditions. Radiosondes (top) consist of balloons with automatic instruments and a radio transmitter attached to them. The transmitter sends back readings from the upper air. In mercury barometers (centre) the greater the 'weight' of air, the higher the mercury is pushed up the tube. The aneroid barometer (bottom) is a metal box, which expands and contracts as the air pressure changes. This makes a pointer move.

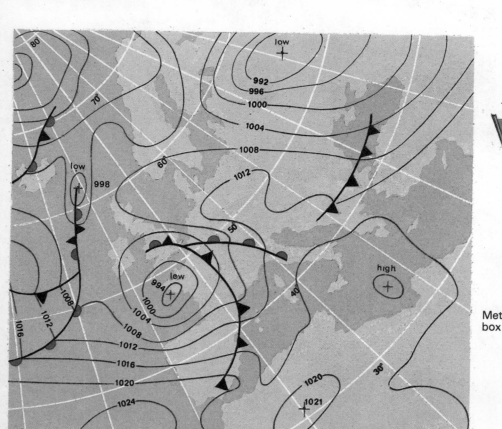

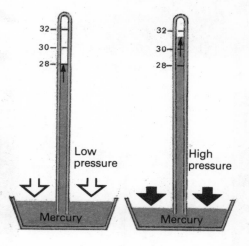

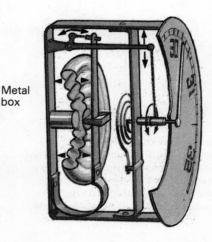

Metal box

# Fossil Fuels

A fuel is something that can be burned to give heat, light or power. It is a store of energy. The energy came in the first place from the Sun. Plants gather energy from the Sun. Oil, gas and coal were formed from plants that lived millions of years ago. They are called *fossil fuels*.

Drilling for oil is a very costly operation. First of all, the oil has to be found. Geologists spend a long time examining the layers of rock under the land or under the sea-bed. When they think there may be oil, an exploration well is drilled. If oil is found, then several more wells are drilled to find out if there is enough oil to justify a full-scale operation. A production platform is put in place, and only then does the valuable oil start to flow. In the stormy North Sea, the platforms may be in 300 metres of water. The oil itself can be 3000 metres below the sea-bed.

Mud tank

As the drill chews into the rock, special 'mud' is pumped down the pipe. The mud comes back up to a tank, where it is cleared of debris. The mud keeps the drill cool and coats the inside of the drilled hole.

## How Coal is Formed

Like oil, coal is formed from living things. It started off millions of years ago as trees and plants in ancient forests. The forests slowly sank into swamps and were covered by layers of mud which later became solid rock. The pressure of this rock and the heat from the Earth began to change the plant remains.

The first stage in the formation of coal can be seen in some wet moorlands and bogs. There decaying plants form *peat,* a substance that can be cut and dried to make fuel that burns.

If peat is left in the ground for long enough it becomes *lignite* or brown coal. As more millions of years go by, the coal grows into *bituminous* coal, the black stuff we burn. The last stage in coal formation is *anthracite,* a shiny black rock that is clean to handle. Anthracite is almost pure carbon.

## How Oil Forms Underground

The oil we use today was probably formed from decayed plants and animals that fell to the ocean floor 500 million years ago. Slowly, over thousands of centuries, the remains of the plants and animals were covered by layer upon layer of sand and mud. The pressure of these layers caused great heat. This heat, combined with chemical action, changed the ancient remains into the substances we call oil and gas. As more time went by, the oil and gas seeped slowly upwards through soft rock. After a while, they reached solid rock and they could go no further. They were in a *trap,* in which collected oil, gas and water. It is these traps which today's oilmen search for.

## All Kinds of Oil

Petroleum from the ground is often called 'crude oil' because it is a complicated mixture of chemicals that has to be sorted out before we can use all the materials in it. This sorting out is done at an oil refinery. A refinery is a maze of steel towers and pipes, but among the main pieces of equipment are tall *fractionating columns.*

Crude oil is heated to a vapour in a furnace. A pipe carries the vapour to an entrance near the bottom of the column. Inside the column, trays are arranged one above the other (see below left). The trays are hottest at the bottom and coolest at the top of the tower. As the oil vapour rises, it passes through holes and is caught by *bubble caps* like upside-down cups (see inset below). The caps force the vapour down again through liquids that have already condensed in the trays. This makes more of the vapour condense.

The various oil products condense to liquid at different temperatures. The heaviest liquids collect at the bottom of the tower – substances such as asphalt for road-making. Above this comes diesel oil, and above this again paraffin for jet planes and home heaters. Near the top appears petrol for cars, while right at the top is gas for cooking and heating.

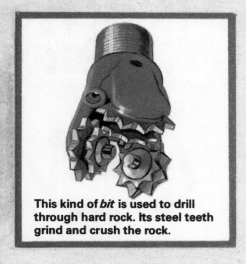

This kind of *bit* is used to drill through hard rock. Its steel teeth grind and crush the rock.

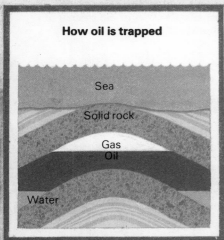

How oil is trapped

Sea

Solid rock

Gas

Oil

Water

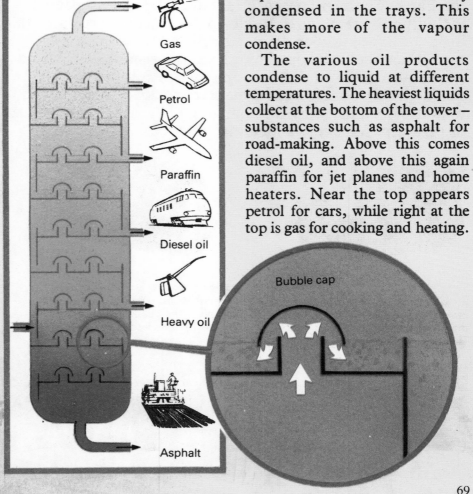

Gas

Petrol

Paraffin

Diesel oil

Heavy oil

Asphalt

Bubble cap

# Rocks and Minerals

Much of the Earth is rock. Mountains and hills are made of rock. The soil is mostly fine rock particles. Stones and pebbles are small pieces of rock. And all the rocks in the Earth's crust are made up of substances called minerals. There are thousands of different minerals and, like all substances, minerals are built up from chemical elements. There are only about a hundred elements – substances such as oxygen, iron and carbon. Most minerals are made up of mixtures of several elements. But a few have formed from only one element. Diamond, for example, is a pure form of carbon.

The most common elements in the Earth's crust are oxygen and silicon. Quartz, the most common mineral, is a mixture of these two elements.

## The Three Types of Rock

There are three main types of rock in the Earth's crust. They are called *igneous, sedimentary* and *metamorphic* rocks. Igneous rocks formed from hot molten material from inside the Earth. Sedimentary rocks are made up of tiny particles including the remains of fossils of microscopic creatures that lived in the sea millions of years ago. As these creatures died, their shells dropped to the sea floor and piled up and were squeezed until they became rock. Limestone, sandstone and chalk are sedimentary rocks. Metamorphic rock has been made by the changing of existing rock by heat or pressure. Marble is a metamorphic rock.

Chalk is a soft, white limestone. It was formed as mud on the bottom of an ancient sea. Chalk consists mainly of tiny shells and calcite crystals.

Sandstone is a common sedimentary rock. The wearing away of sandstone makes up a large part of our beaches. The main ingredient in sand is quartz.

Conglomerate is a mixture of rock fragments cemented together by finer particles. The pebbles in conglomerate are any hard rock such as flint or quartz.

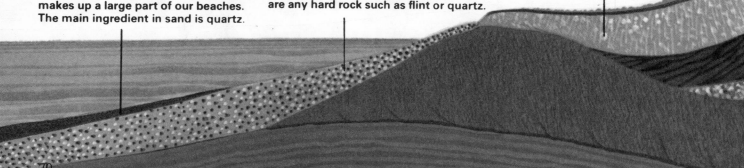

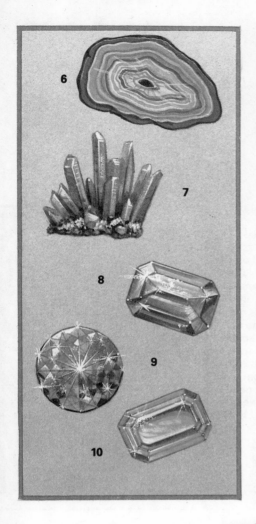

6

7

8

9

10

## Minerals

The panels on the left show some of the many minerals that are found in the crust of the Earth. The minerals in the far left panel contain metals. Minerals that contain sufficient metal for it to be extracted are called ores. The minerals in the near left panel include semi-precious stones and gems. Most of them do not contain metals.

The minerals pictured are: (1) Malachite, an important and beautiful ore of copper; (2) Galena, the chief ore of lead; (3) Wulfenite, a strikingly coloured ore of the valuable metal molybdenum; (4) Zincite, an ore of zinc; (5) Iron pyrites, also known as Fools' gold because its colour has led prospectors in the past to believe they have struck gold; (6) Agate, an attractive form of quartz; (7) Quartz crystals; (8) Amethyst, another form of quartz, widely used in jewellery; (9) Diamond, an extremely pure form of carbon; (10) Emerald, an extremely complex mineral containing beryl and aluminium. The last three minerals are shown cut and polished as they are normally seen in jewellery.

Fossil prints left in ancient rocks tell the scientists much about the past. This is a fossil of a fern plant that lived about 250 million years ago.

Granite is the most common igneous rock. It is made up mainly of quartz crystals.

Slate is a common metamorphic rock. Look at a piece of slate and you will see signs of the great pressure that formed it.

Basalt is crystallized lava that once poured red hot from a volcano.

Volcano

71

Above: A horse painted on the wall of Le Portel Cave, in France, 20,000 years ago.
Right: Some of the simple stone tools made by Stone Age men. They include spears, an axe, a hammer, a scraper, and a needle made of bone.

# The First People

Man and the apes are descended from a common ancestor that lived many millions of years ago. Man-like creatures, hominids, have been roaming the Earth for more than two million years. The oldest remains of Man have been found in Africa.

Modern Man, often called Cro-Magnon Man, from a cave in France where his skeletons were first discovered, came into Europe from the East about 40,000 years ago. Nobody knows for certain when these people first lived, or where. For about a hundred thousand years before this, another group of early people lived in Europe. They were the Neanderthal Men, named after a valley in Germany where they were first identified. Neanderthal Man was probably the first cave-dweller. He was a heavier, clumsier person than modern Man, but he had a large brain, he made tools and hunted, and he buried his dead with elaborate ceremonies.

All these early people are often called Stone Age people, because they made nearly all their tools and implements from hard stones, such as flints. A flint knife can be sharp enough to cut up raw meat easily. Using flint scrapers, Stone Age Man made other tools from wood, bone, and the antlers of deer.

**Early Man lived in caves. He hunted animals such as deer for food, and he knew how to make fire. He often had to fend off animals such as the great cave bear.**

**Neanderthal Man**

**Modern Man**

**Chimpanzee**

# The Ancient World

**Great Wall of China**

**Ziggurat at Ur**

Civilization is a word which means 'living in a city'. The first cities grew up in the Fertile Crescent, an area which ran northwards from the Persian Gulf, through present-day Iraq and round to Egypt.

The earliest civilizations were those of Sumer, Babylonia and Assyria, all in Iraq. The ruins of many of these cities have been found, such as those of Ur, birthplace of Abraham. These cities had *ziggurats*, great towering temples. The ancient Egyptians carried the ziggurat idea further by building pyramids, huge stone structures which served as tombs.

**A debate among a group of Greek philosophers**

**Bull-leaping at Knossos, in Crete**

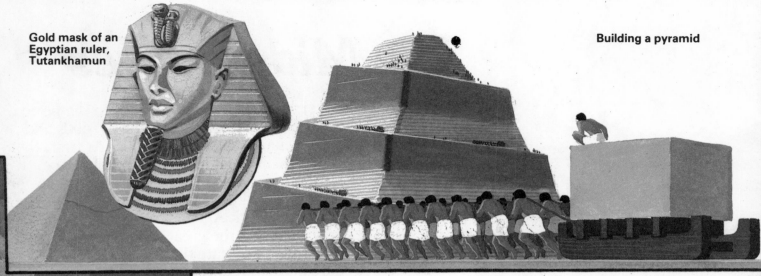

Gold mask of an Egyptian ruler, Tutankhamun

Building a pyramid

Ancient writing

A Grecian urn

Civilization spread gradually northwards through Palestine and the Bible lands. The first civilization in Europe was that of the Minoans, who lived on the island of Crete in the Mediterranean. They are famous for the Minotaur, a mythical monster, and for the dangerous sport of bull-leaping – jumping over a bull by holding on to its horns. The Cretan civilization was closely connected with that of mainland Greece. The Greeks were very clever people. They included some of the greatest architects and sculptors the world has ever known, and also some of the finest thinkers. *Philosophy*, the science of thought, and *democracy*, government by the people, were both evolved by the Greeks.

The Romans, originating at Rome in Italy, were mighty soldiers and conquerors. They built up an empire covering a large part of Europe and North Africa. They were fond of sports such as chariot races, and fights between men known as gladiators. The Chinese civilization is also very old. The Chinese built their Great Wall to keep out invaders at about the time the Romans were creating their empire.

Roman chariot race

The Grecian statue of Venus

75

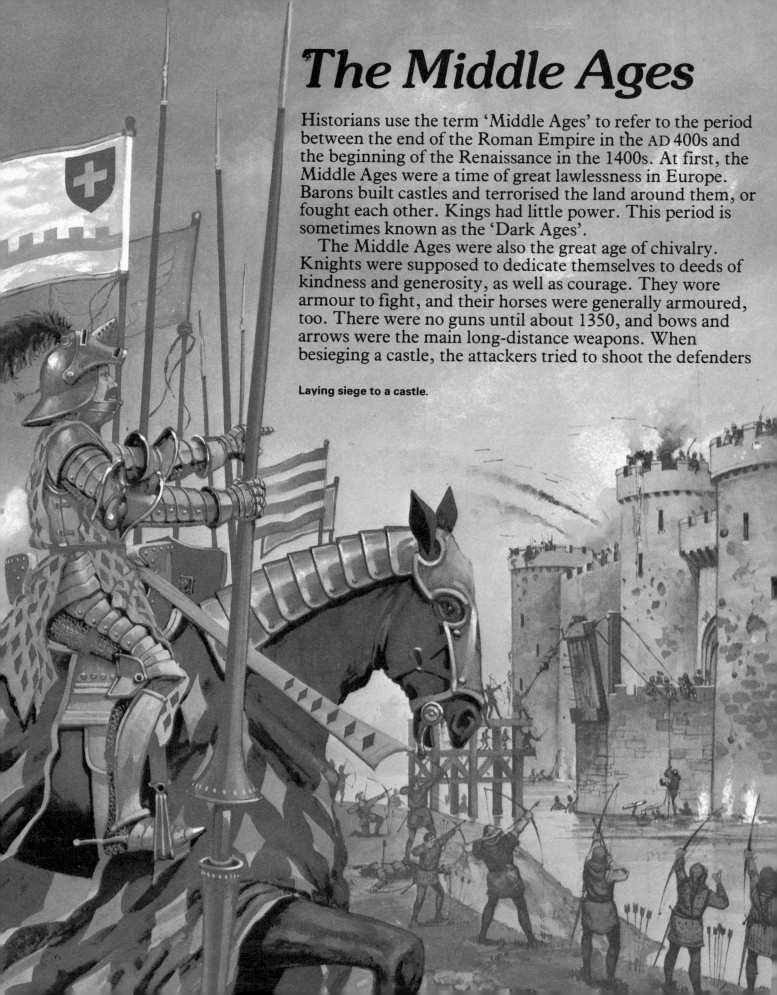

# The Middle Ages

Historians use the term 'Middle Ages' to refer to the period between the end of the Roman Empire in the AD 400s and the beginning of the Renaissance in the 1400s. At first, the Middle Ages were a time of great lawlessness in Europe. Barons built castles and terrorised the land around them, or fought each other. Kings had little power. This period is sometimes known as the 'Dark Ages'.

The Middle Ages were also the great age of chivalry. Knights were supposed to dedicate themselves to deeds of kindness and generosity, as well as courage. They wore armour to fight, and their horses were generally armoured, too. There were no guns until about 1350, and bows and arrows were the main long-distance weapons. When besieging a castle, the attackers tried to shoot the defenders

**Laying siege to a castle.**

The Black Death, an epidemic of bubonic plague, swept Europe in the 1300s, killing one person in four.

**Below:** When the lord of the manor was away at the wars he left his estates in the charge of a reeve, or bailiff, who dealt with the peasants and other workers.

**Bottom:** The 'Mona Lisa' is a painting by Leonardo da Vinci, one of the greatest artists of the Renaissance. It is now in Paris.

on the walls, and to throw up ropes with grappling irons so that they could climb the walls. The defenders responded by dropping rocks and boiling oil on their assailants.

In many countries of Europe, people lived under the feudal system, a term which comes from the word 'feu' meaning fee or services. The system worked as follows: the king held all the land, and gave some of it to his barons in return for military service in time of war. The barons let some of their land to knights or lesser nobles on the same terms, and so on down the line to ordinary peasants – small farmers. There were also serfs, who had no land and were virtually slaves. In later times, the military service gave way to a payment of money, which the king could use to hire soldiers when he needed them. The chief landowner of an area was called the Lord of the Manor.

## The New Age of Learning

Very few people could read or write outside the Church. Learning was kept alive by the monks and priests, who also made copies of all books, because there was no printing in those days.

By the end of the Middle Ages things were changing rapidly. Scholars in Italy became interested in the work and learning of classical Greece and Rome, and so began the Renaissance – a word which means 'rebirth' and describes the renewal of interest in learning. It was helped by the invention of printing in the 1440s, which enabled books to be more widely available. New ideas in art and architecture were developed, too.

# Explorers

We owe our knowledge of the world today to the courage and endurance of the men who set out to explore the unknown. Some of the earliest explorers were the boldest because they had the greatest fears, such as Bartholomeu Dias, whose crew thought they would sail over the edge of a flat Earth. Courage and endurance are still needed, as shown by the adventures of John Blashford-Snell and a British-American party who fought their way through the swamp and jungle of the Darien Gap in Central America.

## NOTABLE DATES IN EXPLORATION

**300 BC** Pythias of Massilia was the first Greek to explore beyond the Mediterranean. He reached England.

**AD 629–643** The Chinese philosopher Hsüan-tsang explored central Asia and India.

**1000** Viking Leif Ericsson visited the shores of North America.

**1271–1295** Venetian merchant Marco Polo travelled to China, and from there explored Burma and India.

**1325–1349** Moroccan lawyer Ibn Battuta explored East Africa, the Middle East, India, Sri Lanka and China.

**1487–1488** Portuguese navigator Bartholomeu Dias became the first European to sail round the Cape of Good Hope.

**1492** Italian navigator Christopher Columbus discovered the West Indies.

**1498** Portuguese navigator Vasco da Gama made the first sea voyage from Europe to India.

**1499** Italian merchant Amerigo Vespucci discovered the mainland of America, now named after him.

**1519–1521** Hernán Cortés, a Spanish adventurer, explored and conquered Mexico.

**1519–1522** An expedition led by Ferdinand Magellan, a Portuguese navigator, made the first round-the-world voyage; Magellan died on the voyage, which was completed by Juan Sebastián del Cano.

**1531** Francisco Pizarro, a Spanish adventurer, explored Peru.

**1541** Hernando de Soto, a Spaniard, discovered the Mississippi River.

**1606** Dutch navigator Willem Janz became the first European to sight Australia.

**1642** Abel Janszoon Tasman, a Dutch explorer, discovered Tasmania and New Zealand.

**1768–1779** In three voyages, English navigator James Cook made the first thorough exploration of the Pacific and Antarctic Oceans.

**1804–1806** American soldiers Meriwether Lewis and William Clark explored the area between the Missouri and Columbia rivers.

**1828–1845** In three expeditions, colonial administrator Charles Sturt explored eastern Australia.

**1849–1873** Scottish missionary David Livingstone explored southern and eastern Africa, discovering the Victoria Falls and several lakes.

**1860–1861** Robert O'Hara Burke and William John Wills made the first crossing of Australia from south to north, but died on the journey back.

**1858** British soldier John Hanning Speke discovered Lake Victoria.

**1876–1877** British-American journalist Henry Morton Stanley explored the River Congo (now the Zaire).

**1878–1879** Swedish scientist Nils Nordenskjöld made the first voyage through the North-East Passage.

**1903–1906** Norwegian Roald Amundsen made the first voyage through the North-West Passage.

**1909** American naval engineer Robert Peary led the first party to reach the North Pole.

**1911** Roald Amundsen led the first party to reach the South Pole.

**1912** Robert Falcon Scott and three other Britons reached the South Pole 39 days after Amundsen, but died on the return journey.

**1958** British geologist Vivian Fuchs led the first crossing of Antarctica.

**1968–1969** British surveyor Wally Herbert led the first surface crossing of the Arctic Ocean.

**1972** British soldier John Blashford-Snell led the first crossing of the Darien Gap, in Panama and Colombia.

Christopher Columbus

Lewis and Clark

Hernán Cortés

**David Livingstone**

**Marco Polo**

Columbus
Magellan
Vasco da Gama
Captain Cook

The map shows the routes of four of the greatest sea voyages. Pictured, clockwise, are Columbus battling across the Atlantic, Livingstone in unknown Africa, Marco Polo in China, Magellan braving the storms in the strait now named after him, Burke and Wills plodding across Australia, Amundsen at the South Pole, Cortés in Mexico, and Lewis and Clark in America.

**Ferdinand Magellan**

**Robert Burke and William Wills**

**Roald Amundsen at the South Pole**

# Ships and the Sea

People first went down to the sea in ships about 7,000 years ago. Since then the seas have provided a major 'highway' for trade between countries. They have also been a battleground on which nations have won and lost empires.

Until the 1800s sails provided the main means of propelling ships. The most magnificent sailing ships were the swift and graceful clippers, which carried tea and later wool between the Far East and Europe. They were full-rigged ships with a huge sail area on three tall masts. In favourable conditions they could reach a speed of 20 knots (37 kilometres per hour).

## The Age of Steam

However, even while the clippers were setting new records in the mid-1800s, the days of sail were numbered. The future lay in the new steamships which were beginning to cross the Atlantic Ocean. In 1845 the 'Great Britain' showed

**SHIPS THROUGH THE AGES**
(drawn to scale)

**Medieval merchant 'cog'**

**Ancient Egyptian trading ship**
15 m

the way ahead. It was an iron steamship propelled by screw propeller. Within a few years metal hulls and screw propellers were standard.

The early steamships had piston steam engines, similar to those used in factories. In the 1890s a new steam 'engine' showed its superiority – the steam-turbine. Steam turbines still power most large ships. Many smaller ships have diesel engines similar to those in trucks, only much bigger.

A handful of ships are nuclear powered. They are mainly naval ships, such as aircraft carriers and submarines. Nuclear power has not yet proved economical enough for merchant ships.

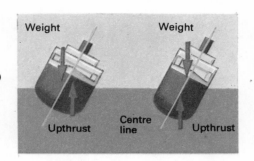

Above: Two main forces act on a ship floating in the water. One is its weight, which acts downwards. The other is an upward force, or upthrust. Ship designers design a ship so that the weight and upthrust act so as to right the vessel when it rolls (left). In a bad design (right) the weight and upthrust act so as to roll the vessel further and make it capsize.

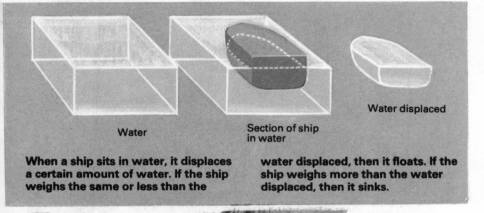

Water

Section of ship in water

Water displaced

When a ship sits in water, it displaces a certain amount of water. If the ship weighs the same or less than the water displaced, then it floats. If the ship weighs more than the water displaced, then it sinks.

Bottom: An interesting comparison of the sizes of ships through the ages. The 'Atlantic' is a giant supertanker and, with a length of 407 metres, is one of the largest ships now afloat. It transports crude oil from the Middle East oilfields.

Mid-19th century clipper

Mid-19th century steamship

1980 Esso 'Atlantic', 407 m

# The Story of Railways

Stephenson's Rocket opened the Liverpool and Manchester Railway in 1830.

The birth of the railways as we know them today can be traced to 1825. In that year George Stephenson built the world's first public railway, the Stockton and Darlington line, in northern England. He also built steam locomotives to run on it, beginning a revolution in transport that spread like wildfire throughout the world.

## Goodbye to Steam

The age of steam on the railways lasted in most countries until the 1950s. Since then steam locomotives have been replaced by diesel and electric locomotives. Steam locomotives were magnificent machines and exciting to watch. But they were very inefficient, dirty and noisy.

The modern diesel and electric locomotives, on the other hand, are efficient, clean and quiet. They can also accelerate more quickly and have a higher top speed. The fastest diesel is British Rail's High Speed Train, which holds the world diesel record of 230 kilometres per hour.

A French electric TGV (Train à Grande Vitesse) holds the absolute rail speed record, with a speed of no less than 380 kilometres per hour. The TGVs now run on the Paris to Lyons line, specially built flat and straight for maximum speed. The other outstanding high-speed railway, the Shinkansen in Japan, also runs on specially built track.

In Canada, Italy, Spain and Britain railway engineers are experimenting with tilting body designs to allow high speeds on existing curved track.

Above: 'Ellerman Lines', a preserved steam locomotive of the Merchant Navy class, built for mainline service in Britain in the 1950s. Weighing some 98 tonnes, it is a Pacific, or 4-6-2 type, having a 4-wheeled bogie in front, 6 driving wheels and 2 wheels beneath the cab. Preservation societies now exist in many countries to restore steam locomotives to their former splendour.

Right: An example of a different kind of railway track, a monorail ('single-rail'). In this particular design, found at Tokyo Zoo, the passenger car is suspended from a wheeled trolley that runs along the overhead rail. In other kinds of monorails, the passenger car straddles the track.

Below: A conventional twin-rail track. The rails are clamped firmly to the sleepers, which are embedded in stone ballast. These days the rails are laid in very long lengths, made by welding short rails together.

Rail

Steel clip

Sleepers

Ballast

Below: Currently the fastest trains in service are the TGVs, which run between Paris and Lyons in France. Like all the latest high speed trains, the TGVs are highly streamlined. They operate at speeds up to 260 kilometres an hour. They are designed as a complete unit, with two power cars and eight trailer cars making up each trainset.

SNCF

# The Motor Car

1902 Panhard Levassor

1909 Rolls-Royce 'Silver Ghost'

1930 Aston Martin

1960 BMC 'Mini'

1982 BMW Mi Coupé

In 1885 a new type of vehicle appeared on the roads in Stuttgart, Germany. It looked much like some of the small steam carriages seen in other towns. But it differed in one important respect – its engine used petrol as fuel. It was the ancestor of the modern motor car. Its inventor was named Karl Benz.

In less than a century the car has developed into our most important form of transport, which greatly affects the way we live. Something like 200 million cars now travel on the world's roads. The latest ones are sleek vehicles, carefully streamlined so that they slip through the air easily. Some are designed for speed, being able to travel over 200 kilometres an hour. Others are designed for economy, being able to travel over 20 kilometres on a litre of petrol. Many are built with the aid of robots.

Cars are a very comfortable and convenient form of transport, but they have their disadvantages. They cause accidents; they burn a fuel obtained from oil, which will soon be in short supply, and they are a major source of pollution. For these reasons car manufacturers are continually redesigning their cars to make them safer, use less fuel, and cause less pollution. They are also experimenting with new kinds of engines that run on steam, hot air, and electricity. These should cause no pollution at all.

## THE FOUR-STROKE CYCLE

Below: Most car engines are piston engines. They contain pistons that move up and down in cylinders. A mixture of petrol and air is burned in the cylinders to produce hot gases. The gases expand and force the pistons down the cylinders to produce power to move the car. The diagram shows how the fuel mixture is taken into the cylinders (1), compressed (2), burned (3), and removed (4), according to a regular cycle, called the four-stroke cycle.

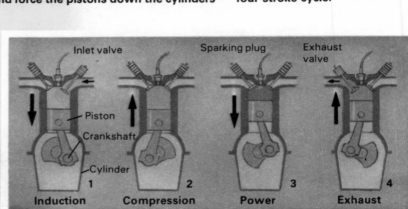

Induction 1   Compression 2   Power 3   Exhaust 4

Inlet valve   Sparking plug   Exhaust valve   Piston   Crankshaft   Cylinder

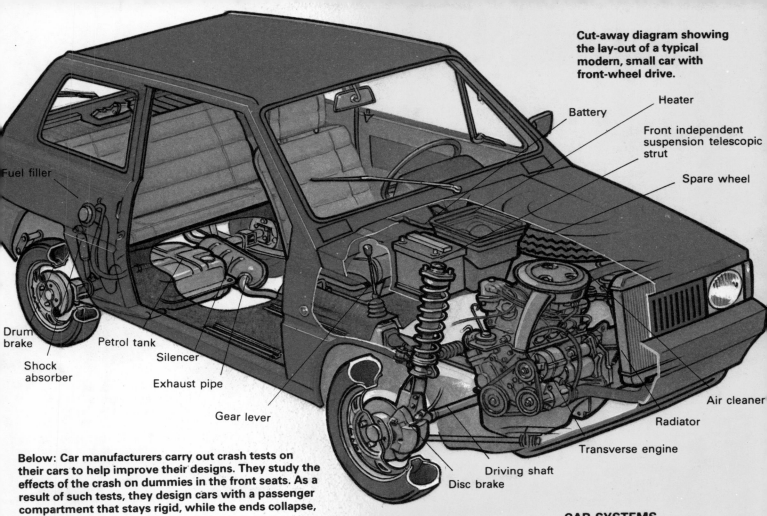

Battery

Heater

Front independent suspension telescopic strut

Spare wheel

Fuel filler

Drum brake

Shock absorber

Petrol tank

Silencer

Exhaust pipe

Gear lever

Disc brake

Driving shaft

Transverse engine

Radiator

Air cleaner

Below: Car manufacturers carry out crash tests on their cars to help improve their designs. They study the effects of the crash on dummies in the front seats. As a result of such tests, they design cars with a passenger compartment that stays rigid, while the ends collapse, or crumple.

Crumple zone

Crumple zone

## CAR SYSTEMS

A car is a most complicated piece of machinery, made up of over 10,000 different parts. For simplicity we can group these parts into a number of different systems. Each system plays a particular part in the operation of the car.

THE ENGINE changes the energy in the fuel into mechanical motion.

THE TRANSMISSION SYSTEM carries, or transmits, the motion from the engine to the wheels. It consists usually of a clutch, gearbox, propeller shaft, and a final drive on the driving wheel axle.

THE STEERING SYSTEM allows the driver to turn the front wheels and so steer the car.

THE BRAKING SYSTEM gives the driver the power to slow down and stop the car.

THE SUSPENSION SYSTEM of springs and shock absorbers cushions the passenger from the effects of bumpy roads.

THE ELECTRICAL SYSTEM provides electricity from a battery to make sparks to ignite the fuel and power the lights, instruments, horn and other equipment.

# Aircraft

Modern hot-air balloon

The highly successful fixed-wing, vertical-take-off Harrier warplane

The original Wright Flyer, 1903

Farman Goliath, 1919

Short Empire flying boat, 1936

Douglas DC-3, 1936. More than 13,000 were built.

The de Havilland Comet 1, 1952, the first jet airliner

The story of Man's conquest of the air began almost exactly two centuries ago, in 1783. In June of that year two French brothers, Joseph and Etienne Montgolfier, launched a hot-air balloon. But such balloons are now used only for sport. Today the skies belong to the aeroplane, commonly just called plane.

The first plane flight took place on 17 December 1903, at Kitty Hawk in North Carolina, in the United States. The plane was built by the Wright brothers, Orville and Wilbur. The first flight lasted for a mere 12 seconds, but it showed the way ahead. In 1909 Louis Blériot flew across the English Channel; ten years later John Alcock and Arthur Whitten Brown made the first non-stop flight across the Atlantic Ocean.

## The Coming of the Airliner

During the 1920s and 1930s regular, or scheduled flights began, at first carrying airmail and later passengers. This was the era of the flying boat. By the end of the 1930s, as the world headed into World War II, a new type of plane was being developed: the jet. After the war the jet plane came into its own, first as a fighter, then as a commercial airliner.

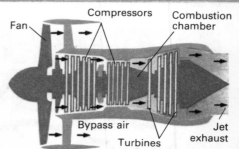

Above: A turbofan engine, used in most airliners. Air is taken into the engine and compressed. Fuel is burned in the compressed air in the combustion chamber. The hot gases produced spin the turbines before emerging as a jet. The by-pass air helps make the jet more efficient.

Below: A plane gets its 'lift' from the shape of its wings, a shape known as an aerofoil.

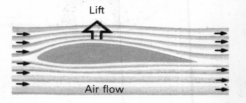

## VERTICAL TAKE-OFF

One drawback of the ordinary plane is that it needs a long runway for taking off and landing. Over the years, different types of aircraft have been developed to overcome this drawback. The most successful has been the helicopter, developed in the 1930s, mainly by Igor Sikorsky in the United States. The helicopter obtains its lift by whirling blades on top of its fuselage. The only successful vertical take-off and landing (VTOL) fixed-wing plane has been the Harrier fighter (left). This moves vertically up and down by deflecting the jet exhausts from its engines.

In the 1960s jet planes became faster and bigger. In 1969 came the maiden flight of the supersonic airliner Concorde, developed jointly by Britain and France. It is still the fastest airliner in service, being capable of a speed of some 2,250 kilometres per hour. This is twice the speed of sound, and is faster than a rifle bullet.

In the same year came the maiden flight of the Boeing 747, the first of the big passenger jets, known as jumbo jets. The Boeing 747 can carry 400 passengers or more, but can operate efficiently only when most seats are filled. Its four engines use a lot of fuel. In recent years, as fuel costs have risen sharply, smaller planes have been developed for more economical airline operation. They include the European Airbus and the Boeing 757 and 767, which all have two highly efficient turbofan engines.

The Anglo-French Concorde supersonic airliner, 1976

The Boeing 747, 1970, the first 'jumbo' jet

Most planes are equipped with an instrument landing system (ILS). This enables a pilot to position the plane accurately for a perfect landing on the runway. It works by means of radio beams.

BAE 146

Glide-path beacon

Localizer beacon

Runway

Inner marker

Middle marker

Outer marker

# Rockets and Launchers

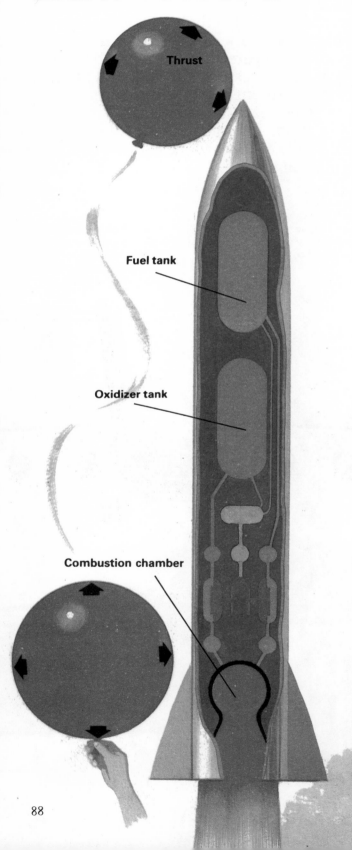

Thrust

Fuel tank

Oxidizer tank

Combustion chamber

Among the most powerful of all engines are the rockets used to launch satellites into space. Yet these rockets work on the same principle as the simple stick rockets we enjoy as fireworks. A fuel is burned in the rocket to produce hot gases, which are then allowed to escape through a nozzle. As the gases shoot backwards, the rocket is thrust forwards.

The substance that propels a rocket is called a propellant. Firework rockets use gunpowder. Space rockets use liquid propellants, such as liquid hydrogen (fuel) and liquid oxygen. They are much more powerful than solid propellants. Because rockets carry oxygen to burn their fuel, they can work in space, where there is no air.

Even so, a single liquid rocket cannot get into space by itself. It has to be helped on its way by other rockets. This is the idea behind the step rocket.

It is a launcher made up of several rockets joined end to end. The bottom rocket fires first and then falls away; the next rocket fires and falls away, and so on. The launcher gets faster and lighter each time and in this way can pick up enough speed to get into orbit.

**Left: The essential parts of a liquid-propellant rocket. The propellants are pumped into the combustion chamber and burned. The hot gases produced escape from the nozzle and propel the rocket forwards.**

**Far left: The action of the balloon can explain how rocket propulsion works. When the balloon is blown up and held (bottom), the pressure on the inside is equal everywhere. When you let go the balloon (top), air escapes backwards through the neck. But the forward pressure remains and propels the balloon. A similar thing happens when the gases escape from a rocket nozzle.**

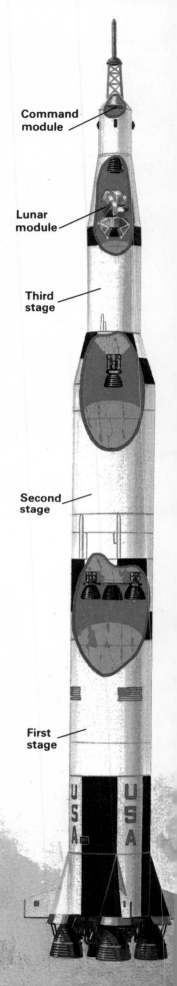

Command module

Lunar module

Third stage

Second stage

First stage

Left: This is the Saturn V/Apollo launcher, the biggest rocket ever launched by the Americans. It was used in the 1960s and 1970s to send astronauts to the Moon. On the launch pad it stood no less than 111 metres high. All that eventually came back to Earth in one piece was the tiny command module containing the three-man crew.

Below: In orbit the space shuttle orbiter opens its cargo-bay doors and launches a satellite.

## Space Shuttle

On April 12, 1981, a new type of space launcher soared into the heavens. It was the American space shuttle. Unlike the launchers before it, the shuttle is a re-usable launch system. It consists of three main parts.

The most important part is the orbiter, which carries the crew. It looks much like a plane and is about the same size as a medium-range airliner like the DC-9. It is some 37 metres long and has a wing-span of some 23 metres. It has three powerful main rocket engines.

The orbiter rides into space on a huge tank, which carries liquid fuel for the main engines. On the launch pad, two solid rocket boosters are attached to the tank. The boosters and the orbiter's main engines all fire together at lift-off. Then the boosters fall away and parachute back to Earth to be used again. Later the fuel tank falls away, but it is not recovered. It is the only part of the shuttle 'stack' that is wasted.

Left: The shuttle blasts off the launch pad in a spectacular fireworks display. In a little over 10 minutes the orbiter is in orbit, travelling at 28,000 kilometres per hour. It has discarded its fuel tank and rocket boosters.

Above: The orbiter takes off like a rocket, but lands like a glider. When it drops from orbit, it is travelling very fast indeed. Gradually the air slows it down to a safe landing speed, and it touches down on an ordinary runway.

# Amazing Machines

Man is not a very strong creature, yet he can move mountains. He has no wings, yet he can fly. He cannot breathe under water, yet he can venture into the ocean deeps. He can even beat the pull of gravity and travel into space, surviving there for months at a time, and return safely. He can do these things – and many more – because he has the brain power to invent machines.

The modern Age of Machines began in the 1700s when several people invented machines to speed up textile making. Then a reliable steam engine was developed to run the machines. This mechanization led to a great change in the way things were made – to an Industrial Revolution.

At the present time we are in the grips of another industrial revolution, brought about by what is called automation. This means the use of machines that work automatically, with little need for human workers. The 'brains' behind the operation of these machines are the 'electronic brains' of the most amazing machine of all – the computer.

## UNDERSTANDING THE COMPUTER

The word computer means calculator. And whatever job they do, computers work by carrying out a series of simple arithmetic calculations on sets of numbers. The numbers can represent all kinds of different information, or *data*. Computers are so marvellous because they can carry out such calculations at incredible speed, often performing hundreds of thousands of operations every second. But they cannot 'think' for themselves. They need a human being to tell them what to do.

The ordinary computer is properly called a digital computer, because it handles data in the form of numbers, or digits. It does not use ordinary decimal digits (0–9), but just the two digits 1 and 0. These are called binary digits, or *bits.*

So all instructions and data must thus be coded into bits before the computer can work on them. The computer does most of this coding itself. But first the computer operator writes his instructions, or program, in a simplified 'language' that the computer can 'understand'. It is called a computer language.

The program and data form what is called the software of the computer. The computer equipment is called the hardware. The software is fed into the computer through an input device such as a keyboard or a magnetic disc or tape unit. Inside the computer it is stored in a memory unit. Calculations are carried out by an arithmetic unit under the control of a control unit. After calculations have been completed, the control unit directs the results to an output device. This may be a video display unit (VDU) like a television screen, or it may be a high-speed printer.

**How a hovercraft works**

Fans blast air downwards

Flexible 'skirt' holds in air

Cushion of air

The hovercraft is equally at home on water as on land, gliding along on a cushion of air. It makes an excellent amphibious landing craft for the armed services. The largest hovercraft, such as the SRN4, are used as car ferries across the English Channel.

Right: The laser produces a narrow beam of pure light containing immense energy. It can be focused into a point of intense heat that can slice through metal like a knife through butter. Lasers have many other uses in the modern world from guiding tunnelling machines to 'playing' the latest compact record discs.

Left: Among the most powerful man-made machines are the turbogenerators used at power stations to produce electricity. The picture shows a massive generator rotor for a hydro-electric power plant.

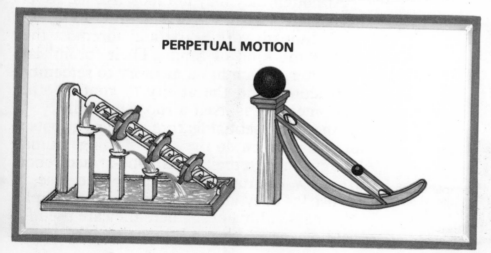

**PERPETUAL MOTION**

Many people have tried to invent machines that, once set moving, would carry on moving by themselves, in endless, or perpetual, motion. The pictures show two ideas. The Archimedean screw raises water as it turns. At the top the water spills out and cascades downwards and turns paddle wheels that turn the screw. It does not work because too much energy is lost in friction. In the ball-and-magnet machine, the idea is that the magnet attracts the ball up the slope. Near the top, the ball falls through the hole and back to the bottom, and is attracted up again. The drawback is that the magnet attracts the ball directly to it.

# Robots All Around

We are now living in a world in which robots are taking over much of the work. Robots make our automobiles, fly our planes, work out our salaries, and prepare our accounts.

But these robots are not mechanical men and women. They do not look like us. They are machines specially built to do some of the things that human beings can. And they are given whatever shape is most suitable. Robots that are built to look like human beings are called androids. These are the kind that usually feature in science-fiction films and comics.

Although they may not look like us, robots need some human features in order to be able to do human work. First and foremost they need some kind of brain. Their 'brain' is a computer, which has a memory to remember instructions and the ability to control other equipment. It is itself a robot machine.

Another essential feature of many robots is an arm that can do the kind of things human beings can with their arms. One-armed robots are now coming into widespread use in industry. They are being used, for example, on car assembly lines. There they are used for welding car bodies and for paint spraying.

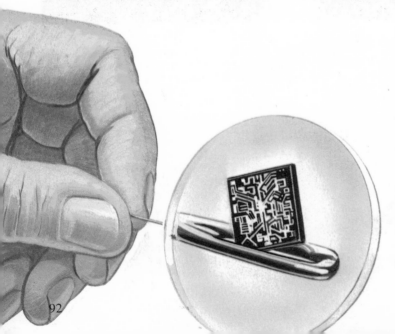

**Below: A tiny crystal wafer provides the 'brainpower' for the new generation of robots. It is the silicon chip, which is so tiny that it can pass through the eye of a needle. Although it is so small, it contains thousands of electronic parts, which turn it into a powerful computer. It can 'remember' instructions given to it and guide the actions of a robot.**

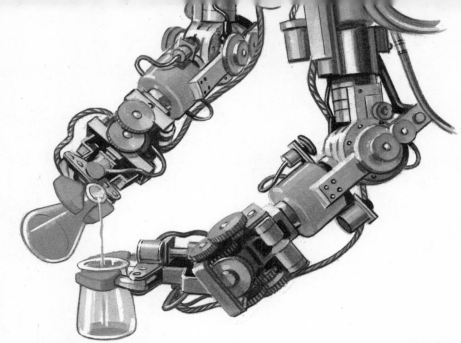

**Right:** It is very difficult to build a robot arm that works as well as the human arm. Many electric motors, joints and levers are required to imitate the actions of the human muscles, elbow, wrist, knuckles and fingers. Usually, however, robot arms do not need to be quite so complicated.

**Opposite:** Robot spacecraft, or probes, venture into the depths of space, where man cannot yet travel. Their instruments and cameras observe and record information about distant worlds and send radio pictures and measurements back to Earth. The picture shows the most successful of all space probes so far, the American-built Voyager. Two Voyager probes were launched in 1977 which have since sent back fantastic pictures of the giant planets Jupiter and Saturn. Voyager 2 went on to send back information about Uranus and Neptune and is now out of our solar system, carrying a message of peace, in case it is ever discovered by beings in a far distant galaxy.

**Below:** This curious beetle-like craft is an experimental robot vessel designed to locate and retrieve objects under water. When working, it supports itself on legs, while its arms carry out the necessary tasks. It is a development of the type of manned submersible craft now being used in offshore oil fields.

The great advantage of robots over human workers is that they can work non-stop for long periods. They never get tired, and always work with the same accuracy. They can also work in conditions that humans could not bear, where it is very hot, very noisy, or where there are dangerous rays. Last but not least, as more robots are built, their cost will come down. Human labor costs, on the other hand, are continually rising.

Although robots are rapidly taking over many jobs in industry, they seem a long way from taking over in the home. The problem is that it would take a very complex and costly robot to perform half the tasks involved in housework.

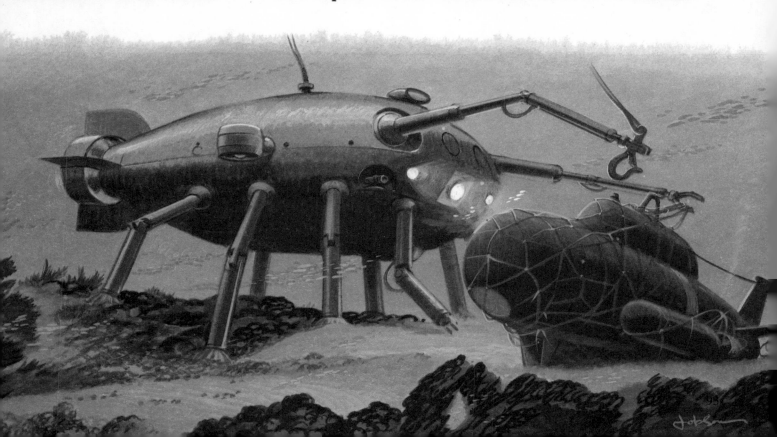